Student
Outcomes
Assessment

Recent Titles in
Contributions to the Study of Education

STUDENT OUTCOMES ASSESSMENT

A Historical Review and Guide to Program Development

SERBRENIA J. SIMS

Contributions to the Study of Education,
Number 52

GREENWOOD PRESS

NEW YORK • WESTPORT, CONNECTICUT • LONDON

Library of Congress Cataloging-in-Publication Data

Sims, Serbrenia J.
    Student outcomes assessment : a historical review and guide to
program development / Serbrenia J. Sims.
        p.   cm.—(Contributions to the Study of Education,
    ISSN 0196–707X ; no. 52)
        Includes bibliographical references and index.
        ISBN 0–313–27591–2
        1. Universities and colleges—United States—Evaluation.
    2. College students, Rating of—United States.   I. Title.
    LB2331.63.S56   1992
    378.1'67—dc20   91–27811

British Library Cataloguing in Publication Data is available.

Library of Congress Catalog Card Number: 91–27811
ISBN: 0–313–27591–2
ISSN: 0196–707X

First published in 1992

Greenwood Press, 88 Post Road West, Westport, CT 06881
An imprint of Greenwood Publishing Group, Inc.

Printed in the United States of America

The paper used in this book complies with the
Permanent Paper Standard issued by the National
Information Standards Organization (Z39.48–1984).

10 9 8 7 6 5 4 3 2 1

Contents

Preface

This book is designed for persons who are interested in the newly developing field of student outcomes assessment at institutions of higher education. More specifically, it is aimed at individuals who are participating in the development, implementation, and evaluation of student assessment programs. Having identified these individuals as the target audience, the purpose of this book is to provide a link between past assessment efforts and decisions about present and future student outcomes assessment efforts at institutions that have only recently showed an interest in the field. For these individuals, this book provides a brief historical review of outcomes assessment and a general guide to designing, implementing, and evaluating assessment programs.

The idea for this book grew out of the author's desire to understand and synthesize the enormous amount of literature that has emerged on the subject of student outcomes assessment. Since 1983, national commissions, the federal government, state governments, accrediting agencies, and countless institutions of higher education have pushed for student assessment initiatives. Initially, it was believed that very little had been written on the subject of student outcomes assessment. However, after reviewing the historical literature, the author concluded that this was not a "new" trend in higher education. In fact, numerous assessment efforts at institutions such as Chicago and Michigan State were conducted over fifty years ago.

Chapter 1 provides several definitions of terms that are commonly used in student outcomes assessment literature. Following the definition section, a review of major actors and the political context for student assessment is presented. In addition the chapter identifies several factors that have contributed to the recent push for assessment. The chapter concludes with a review of the states' and higher education's responses to calls for assessment.

Chapter 2 reviews the history of outcomes assessment testing in the United States. Several landmark studies such as the General College of the University of Minnesota (1932) and the Basic College of Michigan State University (1944) are reviewed. Several special studies are also presented for analysis. And a historical review of the development of national achievement tests is presented.

Chapter 3 focuses on federal and state initiatives that stimulated the recent surge of student assessment initiatives across the nation. More specifically, at the federal level a discussion of the amendments to the *Secretary's Procedures and Criteria for Recognition of Accrediting Agencies* is presented. At the state level a general review of the Education Commission of the States survey of assessment is presented. And finally, a review of assessment efforts in the states of Florida, Tennessee, and New Jersey is included.

Chapter 4 looks at the roots of outcomes assessment as it evolved through accrediting agencies in the United States. The chapter reviews accrediting agencies growth from its inception when it simply provided a definition for college standards to its present emphasis on both input and output measures.

Chapter 5 poses a life cycle concept as typically applied to business organization to aid in the design and implementation of student assessment programs. The life cycle concept suggests that programs are born, grow old, and eventually die if renewal steps are not taken.

Chapter 6 summarizes the main ideas in the book and offers some suggestions for evaluating the effectiveness of the assessment effort at institutions of higher education. The chapter emphasizes the role of evaluation as a feedback mechanism for improving student assessment programs.

The book concludes with an appendix. The appendix offers federal legislation affecting student outcomes assessment and case examples of student assessment initiatives at the state level, the institutional level, and the departmental or program level.

Although the six chapters that make up this book are fairly inclusive of the information available on student outcomes assessment, they are rapidly becoming out of date because of the rapid changes that are occurring in the field. It is impossible to provide a work that will last over the ages. However, it is the author's intention to provide a reference that can be built upon by others.

Finally, I wish to express my appreciation and thanks to Ronald, Nandi, and Dangaia for their patience and forgiveness as I sacrificed a great deal of my time and theirs in the production of this work. In addition, I offer thanks to the reviewer who provided welcomed suggestions for improvement.

I

HISTORICAL PERSPECTIVE
ON STUDENT OUTCOMES
ASSESSMENT

1

Student Outcomes Assessment:
Definitions, Context, and Practices

INTRODUCTION

The concept of student outcomes assessment has recently gained increased attention at the nation's colleges and universities as a result of several national commissions' reports, articles, books, conferences, and legislative mandates. Thus far, at least fifteen states use outcomes measures in their budgeting process. Also, thirteen states have pending legislation, task forces, or commissions responsible for the development of an outcomes assessment policy (Bernardin, 1990). In addition, three-quarters of college administrators report that their institutions are using assessment information in the decision-making process (El-Khawas, 1989). Further, each of the six regional accrediting agencies now require some type of student outcomes assessment in their review process.

This recent attention to the subject of student outcomes assessment leads one to believe that it is a fairly new issue for institutions of higher education in the United States. However, one must realize that the process of determining what students know as a result of their educational experience dates back to the first graduating class of Harvard University in the 1650's, when oral examinations and senior declamations were common.

What makes the recent student outcomes assessment movement significant is that it was primarily stimulated by external sources such as the federal and state governments and national commissions. These sources, seeking accountability for funds and an assurance of educational quality at institutions of higher education, have aided in the shifting of thinking from the quality of inputs into the higher education system to the quality of outputs.

This chapter will introduce the reader to the concept of student outcomes assessment by looking at definitions of terms commonly used in this book and in other student assessment literature. This will be followed by a review of the context for recent assessment initiatives to include factors that influenced the development of student outcomes assessment programs. The chapter will conclude with an outline of the states' and higher education's responses to the calls for assessment results.

Definitions

The terms "measurement," "assessment," and "evaluation" have been voiced on college and university campuses and in state government over the past few years. Frequently in education one word is substituted for another, thereby causing confusion and, in many instances, mistrust and hostility. Drawing a distinction between the terms is often difficult. Lenning (1980) sheds some light on the distinctions. He views measurement as a building-block of assessment and assessment as a building-block of evaluation.

According to Lenning's (1980) observation, "measurement" is the simple process of gathering and quantifying information for future interpretations and serves as the base for the more complex activities—assessment and evaluation. Assessment occurs when measurements are analyzed. And evaluation occurs when judgements are applied to assessment efforts. Therefore, it is impossible to conduct an assessment or evaluation without measurement and analysis.

The term "assessment" at the postsecondary level does not have one unified meaning to its users. To some, it means the assessment of the skills and quality of freshmen entering an institution. This is primarily an assessment of prior learning in preparation for college level course work, and indirectly, of the requirements for remedial programs. In other situations, the concept of assessment means the measurement of college-level learning—of what students learned after one, two, or three years of college. The "rising junior" examination as used in the state of Florida is an example of this concept of postsecondary assessment. And finally, a third meaning, and probably the most widely accepted, is a measurement of college outcomes—of what students learn by the time they graduate. The third interpretation of assessment places emphasis on the outputs or results of education as opposed to the inputs—what goes into the education system (Brown and Faupel, 1986). For the purpose of this book, "assessment" will be defined as the process of gathering and analyzing information about the impact and functioning of undergraduate education (Boyer and Ewell, 1988; Lenning 1980).

The term "assessment" emerged in the late 1930's as a result of research conducted at the Harvard Psychological Clinic by Henry Murray and his associates. Murray used the term to refer to the appraisal of individuals (Hartle, 1985; Lenning, 1980). Because of the work done by Murray, some higher education officials have linked the term "assessment" with the appraisal of individuals (i.e., students, faculty) and the term "evaluation" with group and program appraisals. However, this distinction does not always fit higher education purposes and thus poses problems since the two terms are often interchanged. To help eliminate confusion, for the remainder of this book the term "student assessment" will be used to refer to assessment and evaluation techniques when they are applied to methods of determining how to improve a program (formative) or to determining whether the objectives of a program or an activity have been achieved (summative).

"Formative assessment" efforts are designed for improvement and are usually initiated by a specific internal unit of instruction at a college or university such as a department or school. This is a feedback process based on the assumption that professional educators strive for excellence and that evaluation of their performance is done primarily to improve performance, not to justify termination or program elimination. Benefactors of formative assessment include students, faculty, and entire departments or schools.

Hawthorne (1989) says that in order for assessment information to be useful in a formative way, the following factors are important:

1. Ability to explain the chain of causality: what happened or failed to happen which resulted in outcome Y?
2. Ability to explain the extent to which X leads to Y.
3. Ability to generalize the findings for future applications in the same or different settings (p. 55).

If an assessment program is to be responsive to the three points listed above, the program must look beyond the impacts or outcomes of a program to the processes leading to the impacts/outcomes. Thus, formative assessment processes should be diagnostic and must be aimed at improving student learning by providing continual feedback on academic performance to individual students. Its general aim should be to help faculty identify students' strengths and weaknesses. The information can then be used to design appropriate teaching/learning strategies to support under-prepared students as well as to challenge superior students. In addition, formative assessment efforts can be used diagnostically to help faculty monitor both curricular effectiveness and refinement.

On the other hand, "summative assessment" efforts are designed for accountability and are often stimulated from outside academic units by college administrators or other external audiences such as governmental groups, statehouses, and accrediting agencies that are interested in assessment data to be used in making judgments on the effectiveness of a program (Bloom, Madaus, and Hastings, 1981).

A summative assessment is conducted primarily for one of the following purposes: accountability or resource allocation, certification, selection and placement, or for decisions about pay and promotions (Davis, 1989). Thus the focus of summative evaluation is on the final outcome(s) or impact(s) of a program (Hawthorne, 1989). Little emphasis is placed on the processes that lead to those impacts or outcomes as is the case in formative assessment efforts. Examples given are: information about student progress which can be used to guide admissions decisions or progression to upper-level studies; systematic evaluation of teaching which can inform decisions about faculty salary increases; and information about graduates' job success which can be used to refine curricular innovations (Folger and Harris, 1989).

Oftentimes, both formative and summative practices are conducted on a college campus. Therefore, in order to conserve resources there should be an effort to generate data that will satisfy both efforts while at the same time recognizing the stated purpose for its generation and the audiences who are interested in the results. These audiences are often composed of individuals at all levels of government, in addition to national commissions who initially stimulated the push for student outcomes assessment in the United States.

Major Participants

Several major players have been identified from the assessment literature: at the national level were commissions set up to study the general quality of colleges and universities in the United States. In addition the former Secretary of Education, William J. Bennett pushed for assessment at colleges and universities.

First on the list of commissions that stimulated student assessment is the National Governors' Association. In 1986, the National Governors' Association formed a Task Force on College

Quality designed to focus on how colleges and universities could demonstrate that student learning was occurring. The task force suggested that each college and university implement systematic programs that use multiple measures to assess student learning. The information gathered from these measures should then be used to evaluate the quality of programs at colleges and universities (National Governors' Association, 1986). The National Governors' Association report and its recommendations were influenced by the contents of several other commissions' reports to be discussed below.

The 1983 report *A Nation at Risk: The Imperative for Educational Reform*, issued by the National Commission on Excellence in Education looked at the quality of elementary and secondary education and spurred similar concerns about postsecondary education. The National Institute of Education's report *Involvement in Learning* and the National Endowment for the Humanities report written by William J. Bennett *To Reclaim a Legacy: A Report on the Humanities in Higher Education* also spurred the concern for quality and student assessment in higher education. And finally, the Association of American Colleges report *Integrity in the College Curriculum*, was instrumental in the acceptance of assessment procedures on college campuses. These reports concluded that institutions of higher education needed some method to determine the quality of their students as well as a method for determining curricular reforms.

Another agency that has been involved with student assessment since 1972 is the U.S. Department of Education's Comprehensive Program of the Funds for the Improvement of Postsecondary Education (FIPSE). Currently, FIPSE concentrates on funding projects that focus on assessment of educational outcomes. However, initially FIPSE's emphasis was on the assessment of individual students. But as national interest in student assessment began to grow, FIPSE expanded its emphasis from individual students to the evaluation of programs (Cook, 1989).

In addition to the commissions' reports that stimulated calls for student assessment, one major actor, William J. Bennett was also active in establishing the need for student outcomes assessment. In his November 1984 report, *To Reclaim a Legacy*, William Bennett claimed that colleges and universities were failing to give students "an adequate education in the culture and civilization of which they are members." He also stated that, "Most of our college graduates remain shortchanged in the humanities—history, literature, philosophy, and the ideals and practices of the past that have shaped the society they enter" (Bennett, 1984, p. 1). The report recommended that all students encounter a "core of common studies" to include an understanding of Western civilization; several masterworks in English, American, and European literature; proficiency in a foreign language; and familiarity with non-Western cultures. In addition to this initiative, Bennett continued to push for curricular change.

In October 1986 at Harvard University's 350th anniversary celebration, Bennett (before becoming Secretary of Education) accused colleges and their representatives of having narrow interests in obtaining federal dollars for their institutions, while saying little about other aspects of higher education—such as "purpose, quality, curriculum, and the moral authority and responsibilities of universities" (Bennett, 1986, p. 27–31; Palmer, 1986, pp. 1, 27). In addition to the above accusations, Bennett also charged that colleges and universities often failed to make sure their students actually learned anything before they graduated.

These accusations caused an uproar in the higher education community. College and university officials took immediate offense to Bennett's accusations, calling them superficial because they were based on opinion and did not take into account many important facts about the condition of higher education in the United States (Bok, 1986; Palmer, 1986). Nevertheless, Bennett's comments and the national commissions' reports caused many to question the level of governmental involvement in the affairs of institutions of higher education and thus redefined the context for student outcomes assessment.

Context: Institutional Autonomy versus Political Accountability

The concepts of autonomy and accountability served as the context for arguments on external intervention via assessment and accountability measures in the affairs of institutions of higher education. "Autonomy" in higher education has been defined as the power of a university or college to govern itself with a minimum of outside controls. On the other hand, the term "accountability" is defined as the condition of being held responsible and answerable for the quality and efficiency of specified results or outcomes of an activity over which one has authority (Adelman and Alexander, 1982). The question then becomes, Accountable to whom?

Some feel that institutions of higher education need to be more accountable to the public, government, and themselves. In the introduction to *Evaluating Institutions for Accountability* (1974), editor Howard Bowens states that the increase in demand for accountability is caused by a frustration over rapidly increasing costs and a lack of confidence in institutions of higher education. Bowens also states that accountability:

is the expression of a wish—felt by many public officials, donors, and the general public as well—that the increasing sums laid out for public services ought to be justified by reliable estimates of the outcomes (Bowens, 1974, p. xi).

Accountability is thus closely related to concepts such as program budgeting, cost-benefit analysis, cost-effectiveness, and social indicators that are traditionally associated with private business practices. Nevertheless, the present demand for accountability in higher education requires that the nation's colleges and universities demonstrate that they are providing promised results in an efficient and effective manner. Therefore, student assessment data as a method of outcomes measurement must be collected and publicly disclosed as evidence of the results of a college education.

According to Bok (1979), "The problem is where to draw the line. How much autonomy should universities have in carrying out their academic functions? Under what circumstances may the government intervene? And when the government acts, what methods of regulation should it employ to achieve its ends with minimum damage to the academic enterprise?" (Bok, 1979, p. 82). These questions have been asked throughout history and varying answers have been proposed.

Traditionally, academe has been immune from the pressures of government intervention. Academic independence and diversity have been highly prized and protected values. However, due to heavy reliance on government funding, legal principles permitting the government to insist on institutional accountability and the right to participate to an increasing degree in the academic process were established. According to Cowan (1984), once the principle that government funding also allows government regulation was well established, it was difficult to contain. Even those institutions that decided to forego governmental assistance found themselves unable to disentangle themselves. Once the legal basis for government's intrusion into academic affairs was established there seemed to be no limit to the scope of such regulation. Wildavsky (1979) warned that governmental intervention is incremental— that is, once a base for intervention has been established it is built upon year after year until there is little to no autonomy for the regulated institutions.

Initially, according to Nathan Glazer (1979) government regulation of higher education was benign in its origins and the attitude of faculties had been that of approval. The federal government's involvement with higher education had nothing to do at the beginning with any sense on anyone's part that there were abuses to be controlled. Rather higher education was seen as a good thing. It was valuable for personal advancement, and so access to higher education was considered a suitable reward for veterans. Thus we had the GI Bill and the payment of World War II veterans' tuition. With the launching of Sputnik and the ensuing technology race, it was widely accepted that institutions of higher education could advance America's research capability and achievement. And so there was a second major government involvement: funding of research on American campuses. And it continued from there (Glazer, 1979).

One might ask, How did it happen that higher education came to be viewed by government with suspicion and hostility? Glazer identifies three routes to this final result: (1) real abuses developed as government contracted with higher education for services; (2) the explosion of social regulation such as racial and sexual discrimination; and (3) a real suspicion of and hostility towards higher education institutions that developed among some important opinion-making sectors which represented one or another organized sector of the population and which were ready to appeal to the courts to impose on agencies their particular views of the proper function of regulation (Glazer, 1979). In addition to these concerns, the growing emphasis on increased efficiency and cost-effectiveness in both public and private businesses had its effects on higher education. As higher education increased in size and complexity more money was needed to support its functions. This call for additional funding prompted both the state and federal governments to scrutinize the outputs of the higher education system. In addition to financial concerns for accountability, other historical factors were also important to the recent stimulation of interest in student outcomes assessment.

Assessment throughout History

Student assessment initiatives and the corresponding debate over governmental control of educational accountability has been waged throughout the history of colleges and universities. Early nineteenth-century American colleges employed comprehensive examinations in the form of senior declamation at the end of their baccalaureate studies to prove that they were indeed intelligent individuals capable of performing in society. However, as student enrollment and college courses within curricula increased at the end of the nineteenth-century and early twentieth-century it became difficult to conduct comprehensive examinations on each graduating student. To alleviate this problem the common practice of assigning a credit hour to courses was begun. Once total passed credits totaled 120 or higher a degree was awarded (Hutchings and Marchese, 1990).

The above practice came under fire from reformers such as Abraham Flexner who argued that the quality of college degrees had been lost and thus pushed for the reinstatement of comprehensive examination during the early 1930's. This was only one instance when attention to quality and consolidation resulted in the push for some method of student assessment. Resnick and Goulden (1987) identify two periods of history, 1918–1928 and 1952–1975 (these two periods will be discussed in more detail in chapter 2), when enrollment and curricular expansion stimulated calls for consolidation and assessment of educational quality. These historical antecedents along with more recent factors are once again sounding the calls for student assessment.

FACTORS INFLUENCING THE DEVELOPMENT OF ASSESSMENT PROGRAMS

Measuring student achievement has become an important and controversial part of the educational policy aspect of higher education. Faculty have historically evaluated students through a variety of mechanisms such as oral and written examinations in almost all courses to determine students' grades and whether or not course objectives are being met (SCHEV, 1986; Ewell, 1987).

Not only are students assessed by the faculty at colleges and universities, but the colleges and universities themselves are also assessed. Six regional accrediting agencies function to measure the overall effectiveness of the institutions. Also, over 150 professional accrediting bodies look at specialized programs (ranging from agriculture to nursing education) on these campuses. And many states have a variety of mechanisms such as coordinating bodies that try to keep collegiate programs well-balanced (Harcleroad, 1980). From this perspective, higher education in America is highly assessed. Yet over two-thirds of the states have instituted legislation to aid in the assurance of quality higher education within their borders.

One might ask, Why has assessment recently become so visible and controversial? Some feel that the reasons for the current infatuation with assessing undergraduate education is not clear since faculty have been evaluating students in their individual courses throughout the history of higher education. However, others argue that the recent interest in assessment goes beyond faculty evaluation and is the result of several factors, the first of which is the perceived weakness of the curriculum at institutions of higher education.

Perceived Curricular Weakness in Higher Education

Throughout the history of American higher education the internal debate over the proper balance between specialized courses and liberal education within the college curriculum has been waged. Some contend that the curriculum on college campuses is uneven, lacks overall coherence, and reflects very little of what students are actually learning. Others argue that the college curriculum is merely a reflection of changes in society and thus, is a reflection of the desires of business, students, and the college community. Nevertheless, the push for assessment on college campuses has been viewed as a reaction to "shoddy," "lenient," "out-of-date" instructional practices that began on college campuses in the early 1970's (Rossmann and El-Khawas, 1987, p. 4).

The specialized versus liberal education debate resurfaced during the years 1979–1981 and was further fueled by the release of three national commissions' reports: *A Nation at Risk, Involvement in Learning,* and *To Reclaim a Legacy.* These reports called attention to deficiencies in three basic areas of undergraduate study: the humanities, foreign languages, and international studies (Bennett, 1984). The reports focused broadly on the perceived weaknesses in the undergraduate curriculum, and sometimes, blamed shortcomings on excessive responses to student pressure for curricular flexibility. As a result a select committee of the Association of American Colleges in January 1982 began the Project on Redefining the Meaning and Purpose of Baccalaureate Degrees (Bennett, 1984). Following closely behind the desires for curricular change were changing economic trends in the work place that required a more flexible perspective of college curricula.

Trends in the Workforce

Another explanation for the increasing emphasis on student assessment is the change in the American economy. Packer (1989) reports that between 1955 and 1970 the number of workers and their productivity contributed almost equally to an economic growth of about 3 percent annually. However, around 1973 productivity growth fell by more than half. In order to compensate for this loss in productivity more workers from the baby boom era were embraced by the nation's workplaces. However, with the decline in baby boomers and thus the number of workers available, employers have had to compete for help in a work place that has become increasingly more technology-oriented. Employees are expected to have good reading and mathematical skills and the ability to handle more complex tasks than previously required (Rossmann and El-Khawas, 1987). Therefore, both the secondary school system and the nations' colleges and universities are under increased pressure to respond to the real needs of the workplace.

Political Accountability

As money became tighter in the 1970's due to double digit inflation and oil embargoes, institutions of higher education argued that they should be funded because their end products— well-educated students—would increase the economic base of the states and thus the United States. Fueled by events such as troubled state economies, economic development initiatives, revenue sharing, and cuts in federal spending, states began to take a more serious look at how money was allocated and spent (Rossmann and El-Khawas, 1987). Thus, from a consumer protection standpoint the government began to ask for proof.

In addition to the problems created by economic pressures on both state and federal government, Rossmann and El-Khawas (1987) identified political platforms as a second political stimuli for student assessment at the college level. They suggest that since many political leaders found perceived inadequacies in elementary and secondary education to be an effective political issue, they simply shifted their focus to higher education and began to ask similar questions.

Elementary and Secondary Reform

After the release of *A Nation at Risk* in April 1983, state officials began to ask questions concerning the quality of postsecondary education. *A Nation at Risk* was released by the National Commission on Excellence in Education and stated that high school graduates emerged from school without the necessary knowledge and skills needed for college and the work force. These young people were therefore deprived of the privileges of society. This report sounded the alarm for elementary and secondary education reforms and caused those responsible for colleges and universities to start asking similar questions about higher education.

STATES RESPOND TO ASSESSMENT/ACCOUNTABILITY PRESSURES

States have responded differently to the perceived need to institute some form of student assessment. New Jersey instituted the first state-wide program of student assessment designed to test entering students for basic college skills. Georgia followed with a basic skills test for rising juniors. Florida mandated both an exam for entering college students and rising juniors. Tennessee stepped forward with a required entry level test and financial incentives for institutions to assess their two-year and four-year outcomes. In other states, however, institutions have been encouraged but not required to develop student assessment programs. Virginia is distinctive in that it has charted a middle course: it has mandated student assessment but has allowed the individual colleges to develop or choose those assessment methods most appropriate to their very diverse characters and missions (SCHEV, 1987).

Virginia's student assessment policy is important because it serves as an interesting example for other states that have not yet instituted student assessment legislation. By mandating student assessment and then allowing the diverse institutions to develop their own methods of assessment, Virginia's policy allows institutions to maintain a high level of autonomy, thereby reducing fears of governmental control.

Virginia's policy was developed after careful consideration of the advantages and disadvantages of other states' actions. Ideally, it will serve its primary purpose—assessing student achievement—while at the same time maintaining a balance between higher education's need for autonomy and the state's need for accountability of resources. (A historical case of Virginia's student assessment policy formulation process is presented in the appendix.)

HIGHER EDUCATION RESPONDS TO ASSESSMENT/ACCOUNTABILITY PRESSURES

Ideally, the policies and procedures required to reach assessment goals would also aid institutions of higher education in determining whether or not departmental/program, intended outcomes, or educational objectives are being accomplished. Student assessment procedures met with resistance from many institutions of higher education. Some argued that their reputations for excellence, the quality of their entering student body, and the quality of their faculty should exempt them from student assessment procedures. In addition to these arguments, institutions were also resistant because state mandated student assessment procedures were viewed as a threat to campus autonomy. Institutions also feared that student assessment would promote unintended side effects such as "teaching to the test," limiting access of the educationally disadvantaged to a college education, and adversely affecting institutional diversity (Sims, 1989).

These criticisms were being expressed across the nation. For example, in a 1986 survey done by the American Council on Education the following stumbling blocks to assessment were identified: no funds to develop procedures (71 percent); no clear way to evaluate (64 percent); fears about misuse of results (60 percent); lack of faculty support (58 percent); and no good evaluation instruments (57 percent). Because of the traditional hands-off approach that state and federal governments in the United States have employed in relation to their colleges and universities, the changes enacted in the states are all the more exceptional. What factors influenced these decisions to intervene into the affairs of higher education? And what are the intended results of the intervention? These questions are constantly being asked in an effort to assess the quality of higher education in the United States.

SUMMARY

The concept of student assessment or student outcomes assessment has received renewed strength at institutions of higher education across the United States since 1985. This renewed interest is a result of several factors such as calls for curricular renewal and quality by national commissions and former Secretary of Education William Bennett; political accountability efforts; elementary and secondary reform; and changing work force conditions.

Responses to student assessment and corresponding calls for accountability were put in motion almost immediately by the states in an effort to make institutions more accountable for resources and for the quality of students exiting the institution. However, higher education's response was slower, raising the old argument of the extent of public accountability in the light of institutional autonomy. Nevertheless, both summative and formative assessment evaluations of student outcomes are being conducted at a majority of colleges and universities in the United States.

REFERENCES

Adelman, C., and Alexander, R. J. (1982). *The self-evaluating institution: Practice and principles in the management of educational change.* New York: Methuen & Co.
Association of American Colleges. (1985). *Integrity in the college curriculum: A report to the academic community.* Washington, DC: Association of American Colleges.
Bennett, W. J. (1984). *To reclaim a legacy: A report on the humanities in higher education.* Washington, DC: National Endowment for the Humanities.
Bennett, W. J. (1986). Text of Secretary Bennett's address at a Harvard University anniversary celebration. *The Chronicle of Higher Education,* 27–31.
Bernardin, H. J. (1990). Outcomes measurement: A review of state policies toward outcomes measurement in higher education. *The Academy of Management News,* 20(1), 4–5.
Bloom, B. S.; Madaus, G. F.; & Hastings, J. T. (1981). *Evaluation to improve learning.* New York: McGraw-Hill Book Company.
Bok, D. (1979). The federal government and the university. *The Public Interest,* 50, 80–101.
Bok, D. (1986). Text of Harvard president Derek Bok's response to Education Secretary Bennett. *The Chronicle of Higher Education,* 17–19.
Bowens, H. R. (Ed.) (1974). *Evaluating institutions for accountability, New Directions for Institutional Research.* San Francisco: Jossey-Bass.
Boyer, C. M. & Ewell, P. T. (1988). *State-based approaches to assessment in undergraduate education: A glossary and se-*

lected references. Denver: Education Commission of the States.

Brown, G. H., & Faupel, E. M. (1986). *Postsecondary assessment report of a planning conference November 20, 1986*. Center for Education Statistics. Office of Educational Research and Improvement. U.S. Department of Education.

Cook, E. C. (1989). FIPSE's role in assessment: Past, present, and future. *Assessment Update*, 1(2), 1-3.

Cowan, D. (1984). The expanding conflict: Society's demands/academic independence. *Change*, 16(2), 34-39, 54.

Darling-Hammond, L. (1989). Accountability for professional practice. *Teacher College Record*, 91(1), 59-80.

Davis, B. G. (1989). Demistifying assessment: Learning from the field of evaluation. *Achieving assessment goals using evaluation techniques*. New Directions for Higher Education, no. 67. San Francisco: Jossey-Bass.

El-Khawas, E. (1989). How are assessment results being used? *Assessment Update*, 1(4), 1-2.

Ewell, P. T. (1985). *Levers for change: The role of state government in improving the quality of postsecondary education*. Denver: Education Commission of the States.

Ewell, P. T. (1987). Assessment: Where are we? *Change*, 19(1), 23-28.

Finn, C. E. (1978). *Scholars, dollars, & bureaucrats*. Washington, DC: The Brookings Institution.

Folger, J. K., & Harris, J. W. (1989). *Assessment in accreditation*. Sponsored by: A Grant from the Improvement of Postsecondary Education.

Glazer, N. (1979). Regulating business and the universities: One problem or two? *The Public Interest*, 51, 43-65.

Harcleroad, F. F. (1980). *Accreditation: History, process, and problems*. AAHE-ERIC Higher Education Research Report no. 6.

Hartle, T. W. (1985). The growing interest in measuring the educational achievement of college students. In Clifford Adelman (Ed.), *Assessment in American higher education: Issues and Contexts*. Washington, DC: Office of Educational Research and Improvement. U.S. Department of Education.

Hawthorne, E. M. (1989). *Evaluating employee training programs: A research-based guide for human resource managers.* New York: Quorum Books.

Hellriegel, D., & Slocum, J. W. (1989). *Management* (fifth edition). Reading, Massachusetts: Addison-Wesley Publishing Company.

Hutchings, P., & Marchese, T. (1990). Watching assessment: Questions, stories, prospects. *Change,* 22(5), 13–38.

Lenning, O. T. (1980). Assessment and evaluation. In Ursula Delworth, Gary R. Hanson, and Associates (Eds.), *Student services: A handbook for the profession.* San Francisco: Jossey-Bass.

National Commission on Excellence in Education. (1983). *A nation at risk: The imperative for educational reform.* Washington, DC: U.S. Department of Education.

National Institute of Education. (1984). *Involvement in learning: Realizing the potential of American higher education.* Washington, DC: National Institute of Education.

Packer, A. (1989). Preparing the workforce 2000. *Human Capital,* 1(1), 34–38.

Palmer, S. E. (1986). Education secretary calls for fundamental changes in colleges. *The Chronicle of Higher Education,* 1, 27.

Palmer S. E. (1986). Campus officials assail Bennett's attack on colleges; Harvard's Bok calls secretary's analysis 'superficial.' *The Chronicle of Higher Education,* 1, 17.

Rossmann, J. E., & El-Khawas, E. (1987). *Thinking about assessment: Perspectives for presidents and chief academic officers.* Washington, DC: American Association for Higher Education. American Council on Education.

Sims, S. J. (1989). *The origins and development of Virginia's student assessment policy: A case study.* Unpublished doctoral dissertation, The College of William and Mary, Williamsburg, Virginia.

State Council of Higher Education for Virginia. (1986). *The measurement of student achievement and the assurance of quality in Virginia higher education: To the governor and the general assembly of Virginia: Senate document No. 14.* Richmond, Virginia.

State Council of Higher Education for Virginia. (1987). *The Virginia plan for higher education.*

Study Group on the Condition of Excellence in American Higher Education. (1984). *Involvement in learning: Realizing the potential of American higher education.* Washington, DC.

Wildavsky, A. (1979). *Speaking truth to power: The art and craft of policy analysis.* Boston: Little, Brown & Company.

2 ⎯⎯⎯⎯⎯⎯⎯⎯⎯⎯⎯⎯⎯⎯⎯⎯⎯⎯⎯⎯⎯

Historical Review of Student Outcomes Assessment Efforts in the United States: 1918–1952 and 1952–1975

INTRODUCTION

In the recent literature on student outcomes assessment little attention has been given to the history of assessment as it evolved in the United States. Many publications erroneously report that little is known about the outcomes of higher education at the nations' colleges and universities because we simply have not been able to measure them. However, Pace (1984) refutes this argument. He reports that higher education institutions over the years have developed many measures of student outcomes that adequately and accurately assess outcomes. In addition, Lenning (1977) through his work at the National Center for Higher Education Management Systems (NCHEMS) identified over eighty attempts to structure educational outcomes and outcomes related concepts at institutions of higher education. Many of the efforts identified by Lenning (1977) were primarily concerned with developing classifications or models of student outcomes concepts such as educational goals, objectives, and purposes. On the other hand, other efforts focused on the educational outputs themselves and/or the outcomes of those outputs. Some of the areas identified were university based assessment programs, special studies, and national achievement programs.

This chapter will examine the history of student outcomes assessment during two periods of influence: 1918–1952 and 1952–1975 (chapter 3 will examine student outcomes assessment, particularly federal and state initiatives, from 1975 to present). Within these two periods of influence, emphasis will be placed on assessment efforts that fall into the three categories listed above (university based programs, special studies, and national achievement programs). Furthermore, within each category, assessment efforts will be discussed according to their chronological appearance in the literature on outcomes assessment.

The first two periods of assessment history (1918–1952 and 1952–1975) were characterized by major changes in the undergraduate curriculum as a result of internally (internal to the institutions of higher education) motivated demand in response to stressful increases in the numbers of students participating in the higher education system (Resnick and Goulden, 1987). Events that occurred during each period have stimulated a movement for student assessment with the goal of restoring "coherence and substance" to the undergraduate program at college and universities (Resnick and Goulden, 1987, p. 77).

OUTCOMES ASSESSMENT EFFORTS: 1918–1952

The first period of outcomes assessment in higher education was from 1918–1952. During this period the portion of eighteen to twenty-four year olds attending college rose from 3.6 percent to 7.1 percent. The early years of this period were characterized by educators complaining about the incoherence of the curriculum, the low abilities of the students, and the overcrowding of institutions (Resnick and Goulden, 1987). During this period of expansion, Tatlock (1924) complained about the absence of assessment measures that could register the difference between the ideals of college education and the actual gains made by students. Tatlock argued, "There is no opportunity to appraise the student as an entire educated human being" (Resnick and Goulden, 1987, p. 86). In addition, Tatlock bemoaned that the course program was merely "fantastic patchiness which was sometimes ludicrous" (Resnick and Goulden, 1987, p. 80). This and similar complaints impelled institutions to develop holistic and integrative assessment measures such as comprehensive examinations in a student's major field of study. Generally these tests were locally designed and administered by the faculty at an institution. Comprehensive examinations were expected to bring integrity back to major fields of study, increase students' desire to learn, and give students the opportunity to defend their command of a field.

According to Levine (1981), the undergraduate curriculum of this period was similar to today's program blend of free electives, general education requirements, and concentration in a major field of study. The curriculum was also being attacked on the same grounds as today's curriculum—for its lock step approach, over-specialization, eclecticism, and general lack of integrity. The free elective component received more than its share of criticism. The critics suggested four remedies: general education, collegiate education, experiential or life education, and honors and independent study. Two exemplary university-based programs at the University of Minnesota and Michigan State University were developed to address these concerns.

University-Based Centers for Test Development

The purpose of this section is to present in abbreviated form a more complete picture of student assessment initiatives that occurred at colleges and universities from 1918-1952. The two college programs (University of Minnesota and Michigan State University) discussed in this section were only the tip of the iceberg on curriculum experiments in general education and educational outcomes. Other colleges such as the University of Chicago, St. Johns, Bennington, Sarah Lawrence, and Stephens College also rebelled against the conventional curriculum with its excessive fragmentation, its tendency toward undue specialization, and its total neglect of many areas of out-of-school livings (Eckert, 1943).

General College of the University of Minnesota

During the fall of 1932, the Committee on Educational Research at the University of Minnesota established the General College to provide an appropriate type of education for students with moderate academic talents. The needs of this group of students, who were comparatively new to American colleges and universities during the time, did not seem to be met by either the traditional liberal arts curriculum or the various professional schools' curricula (Eckert, 1943). In an effort to determine how to best serve these students the General College of the University of Minnesota committed itself to knowing "what we were getting for what we were doing" (Eckert, 1943). This meant that good, objective comprehensive examinations in selected courses and disciplines had to be designed and conducted to meet this objective.

Before the General College could begin to serve its stated purpose, two inhibitors to change at the University of Minnesota had to be addressed. The first inhibitor was the preconceived notion that higher education curricula tend to grow uncontrollably like a cancer with no established mechanism for course elimination. The second inhibitor was the assumption by instructors that each year's student class is lower in intelligence, enthusiasm for achievement, and interest than the previous class (MacLean, 1943). These barriers were avoided by simply authorizing the General College as a new and independent unit of the University thus allowing the College to develop and expand its curriculum and address students needs as it saw fit.

The General College was faced with four tasks that still plague assessment initiatives today. First, to identify and render as explicitly as possible the goals of the program, so that evaluation could be focused on objectives judged important by those actually responsible for the curriculum. Developing goal statements proved tedious. The first set of statements were deemed too vague and abstract. Suggested solutions were to make the goals quanti-fiable, simpler, less multiple, realistic, and more concrete—many of the same suggestions that are being made in present assessment initiatives (see Farmer, 1988; and Nichols, 1989). Second, to study the kinds of young people served by the college so that any gains they made in knowledge, skill, or appreciation might be interpreted in the light of their characteristics at entrance and the type of education experience the college provided for them. This "value-added" approach to assessment has become associated with Northeast Missouri State University (1974, 1982). Third, to explore the specific character of the changes in students' information, attitudes, and off-campus activities that occur during their attendance at the General College. And fourth, to determine the attitudes of students toward the General College as an institution (Eckert, 1943). Thus the need for reliable and valid student assessment instruments.

The committee experimented with various types of testing procedures in their effort to construct valid and reliable exami-nations in economics, chemistry, biology, and physics. These procedures included: multiple choice questions, matching, his-torical sequencing of events, and applying principles to new situations. In addition, technical concerns about item discrimina-tion, test reliability, and intercorrelations among different parts of a test were considered (Pace, 1984).

According to Pace (1984), test items for these examinations were written and classified for three common types of objectives:

1. acquiring the terminology or vocabulary distinctive to the course,

2. acquiring principles and other factual information, and

3. applying the knowledge of facts and principles to interpret new situations or problems (Pace, 1984, p. 11).

Results showed that these three common objectives were related to one another. In addition, the objective examination in the General College revealed that the difference in scores on post-test examinations were always significantly higher than scores on the pre-test examinations for each course.

Basic College—Michigan State University

In 1944, Michigan State University created its Basic College for freshmen and sophomores and an examiner's office headed by Paul Dressel to work with the faculty in preparing comprehensive examinations for its courses in Effective Living, Biological Science, Physical Science, Social Science, History of Civilization, Literature and Fine Arts, and Written and Spoken English. The examiner's office was administratively independent of the instructional departments and was composed of subject matter experts. These experts were appointed on a full-time basis and were responsible for writing, administering, and scoring examinations in the subject area.

The Basic College and its examiner's office were developed as an administrative arm to make sure that all students shared in a core of learnings as a result of the reorganization of the curriculum at Michigan State. Five objectives of the Basic College were established. The first objective was to provide a common core of learning to be shared by all students regardless of their major or special interest. The second objective was to improve counseling by providing detailed information about individual student's interests, aptitude, and abilities. This gave the students the opportunity while enrolled in the Basic College to choose their fields of specialty based on identifiable interests and to progress at their own rate in accordance with their interests and abilities. The third objective of the Basic College was to recognize in its program the need of those students who did not qualify for a degree. The fourth objective was to recognize students as individuals, varying greatly in experience, education, competence, interests, and aptitudes. This objective placed emphasis on impartial evidence of achievement rather than on completion of a standard sequence of activities.

Although there were several advantages to the Basic College and its examiner's board, such as providing individual case records as needed for adequate counseling of students and promoting greater uniformity and quality in examinations, there were also limitations to the system. Dressel (1949) identified two limitations of the Comprehensive Examination Evaluation Program. First, the uniformity and objectivity of grading was questioned by some who valued emphasis on the development of intangible characteristics such as interests, attitudes, appreciations, beliefs, and values; whereas the Program aimed to separate the measurement of their attainment from the actual grade students were awarded. The second limitation of the Program was the separation of grading from instruction. Faculty reacted negatively to the separation of grading from instruction. They felt that their prestige, power, and authority had been circumvented and their credibility as graders questioned.

Special Studies

In addition to school-based assessment efforts, Pace (1979, 1984) identifies three landmark studies—the Pennsylvania Study, the Cooperative Study in General Education, and the Cooperative Study of Evaluation in General Education—that resulted from the desire to understand students' knowledge attainment during their college experience. These studies or achievement tests reflected subject matter traditionally associated with a college education such as "knowledge and understanding in the sciences, the social sciences, the humanities and arts and with more specific subjects such as economics, chemistry, and psychology" (Pace 1979, p. 9). The first study, the Pennsylvania Study conducted in 1928, 1930, and 1932, tested nearly all the college sophomores and seniors in all institutions of higher education of the state.

The Pennsylvania Study

The underlying purpose of the Pennsylvania Study was to learn what the bachelor's degree "amounts to in terms, first, of clear, available, important ideas, and second, of ability to discriminate exactly among ideas and to use them accurately in thinking. These objects are among the main reasons for acquiring an education and for the existence of educational institutions" (Learned and Wood, 1938, p. 371). In order to achieve this stated goal or purpose, in May 1928, approximately 4,500 (70 percent) graduating seniors from forty-five Pennsylvania colleges took the twelve-hour examination.

At the first administration of the tests in 1928, the examinations were given in four sitting of three hours each. The first sitting contained questions on the physical world, physics, chemistry, astronomy, geology, geography, biology, botany, zoology, and physiology. The second sitting focused on the social sciences as well as statistics, foreign languages, and knowledge of ancient cultures such as Greek and Roman. The third sitting tested knowledge of Western civilization before the Industrial Revolution. The fourth sitting of the examination focused on more recent Western civilizations and topics and knowledge about non-Western civilizations such as Chinese, Japanese, Indian, and Moslem (Pace, 1979).

The highest score of all seniors taking the test was 1,560 out of the 3,200 items on the test. And the average score of all seniors was 570. In general, all groups of students who had less than the statewide average number of related credit hours had average test scores that were also below the statewide average score; and all groups of students who had more than the statewide average number of related credit hours also had test scores that were higher than the statewide average score.

The second administration of the Pennsylvania achievement test was conducted in the Spring of 1930. During this administration, a revised examination was given to college sophomores and to seniors in 1932. The revised tests had the same broad scope and purpose as the original test given in 1930, but the number of items were reduced from 3,200 to 1,882 and the time length was correspondingly reduced to eight hours. Other revisions to the tests included the omission of the foreign language requirement, and the addition of an English and a math test. The remainder of the tests consisted of items on general culture such as the sciences, foreign literature, the fine arts, history, and the social sciences. The examination established the ability to cover a wide variety of information using objective test items such as true/false, multiple choice, and matching. In the Pennsylvania Study's final report emphasis was placed on the range of scores of students in each of the forty-five colleges, the great overlap of the distribution of scores between institutions, and the difference in average scores between the different institutions. The report concluded that during the last two years of college the typical student in the Pennsylvania Study gained significantly in general knowledge measured by these achievement tests, all or nearly all the specific subjects measured by the test (except mathematics) regardless of their major field of study, and gained most on those parts of the test which were most clearly related to the major field. Pace (1979) concluded that students learn what they study, and the more they study, the more they learn.

Cooperative Study in General Education

The Cooperative Study in General Education directed by Dr. Ralph Tyler and under the sponsorship of the American Council on Education was conducted from January 1939 to September 1944, with a primary goal of improving programs in general education in twenty-five participating institutions of higher education. Subsidiary to this goal was the desire to persuade institutions of higher education to implement positive changes in educational practices. Emphasis was placed on the discovery and development of leaders in the various disciplines who were capable of gaining a broader and more realistic perspective of the problems of general education in a college's curriculum. And finally, to promote cooperation among institutions in developing general education programs, institutions were encouraged to interchange results of their experimentation and study to the end that the results of the study would be made available to all American institutions of higher education (Tyler, 1947). This project was a success in that it developed numerous instruments useful in assessing growth in regard to general education objectives at the colleges and universities that participated in the study (Dressel and Mayhew, 1954).

Colleges selected for participation in the study were intended to represent a cross section of American higher education institutions. From the group selected the following types of institutions were represented: land grant colleges; municipal universities; state teachers colleges; independent liberal arts colleges; Catholic colleges; Protestant colleges; traditionally black colleges; four-year womens' colleges; junior colleges for women; and coeducational junior colleges (Tyler, 1947).

Twenty-two colleges originally participated in the study. They were Allegheny College, Antioch College, Ball State Teachers College, Bethany College, University of Denver, Hendrix College, Hiram College, Hope College, Iowa State College, Little Rock Junior College, University of Louisville, Michigan State College, Mills College, Muskingum College, Northwest Missouri State Teachers College, Olivet College, Park College, Pasadena Junior College, College of St. Catherine, Stephens College, Talladega College, and the College of Wooster. During the course of the study the following colleges withdrew: Bethany College, University of Denver, Hiram College, Hope College, Mills College, Olivet College, and the College of Wooster. The following colleges joined later: Centre College of Kentucky, Fisk University, and Macalester College.

Although these colleges had diverse missions they felt that they would benefit from a concerted effort to study many of the problems that they faced. In addition they believed that despite their differences certain basic problems were sufficiently similar to warrant a united effort. By sharing experiences, materials, and ideas, and dividing the labor certain complex problems could be more easily attacked (Tyler, 1947).

The Study was designed to aid in answering the following questions:

- Who should receive a general education?
- What should be the ends of a general education?
- How should the definite objectives be selected?
- What kinds of courses should be offered for general education?
- What content should be included?
- What teaching methods and materials should be used?
- How should achievement be appraised and recorded?
- What characteristics are required of the student personnel and guidance program?
- How should work in general education be organized and administered?
- How should instructors be selected and educated?

Because of the individual emphasis of the study, the results were different for each type of institution that participated in the study.

Cooperative Study of Evaluation in General Education

The Cooperative Study of Evaluation in General Education was initiated in the spring of 1950 to study the evaluation of collegiate general education. The study was sponsored by the American Council on Education and funded by the Carnegie Commission and the participating institutions of higher education. Dressel and Mayhew's (1954) book *General Education: Explorations in Evaluation* summarizes the results of this study. The most significant results of this study were various tests of critical thinking and analysis in the following areas: social science, communications (reading and writing), science, humanities, and a general analysis of the two pervasive objectives—critical thinking and attitudes.

Six objectives of the Study were identified and six committees were set up to accomplish these objectives. The objectives were:

1. "To participate actively as an informed and responsible citizen in solving the social, economic, and political problems of one's community, State, and nation" (Committee on Social Science Objectives)

2. "To understand the common phenomena in one's physical environment, to apply habits of scientific thought to both personal and civic problems, and to appreciate the implications of scientific discoveries for human welfare" (Committee on Science Objectives)

3. "To understand the ideas of others and to express one's own effectively" (Committee on Communications Objectives)

4. "To attain a satisfactory emotional and social adjustment" (Committee on Attitudes, Values, and Personal Adjustment)

5. "To understand and enjoy literature, art, music, and other cultural activities as expressions of personal and social experience, and to participate to some extent in some form of creative activity" (Committee on Humanities Objectives) (Dressel and Mayhew, 1954, p. 12).

6. "To acquire and use the skills and habits involved in critical and constructive thinking" (Committee on Critical Thinking)

The study, originally estimated to take over five years, was modified and compacted into a three-and-a-half-year period. During this time period energy was spent studying objectives, developing evaluation procedures, planning a research design, following a group of freshmen from the beginning of their first year to the beginning of their third year of collegiate study, analyzing data, making implications based on the data, and preparing the final report (Dressel and Mayhew, 1954).

National Testing Agencies and Achievement Tests

Three national testing agencies were significant to measuring student outcomes assessment in the 1940's. One was the Graduate Records Office of the Carnegie Foundation that produced the Tests of General Education. The second was the Cooperative Test Service, best known for the General Culture Tests. The third was the Educational Testing Service which was established in 1948 and took over the cooperative testing program. The Tests of General Education took eight hours to complete and covered general mathematics, physical sciences, biological sciences, social studies, literature, arts, effectiveness of expression, and vocabulary. Each topic specifically related to subject matter of the college curriculum except for vocabulary. On the other hand, the General Culture Tests covered current social problems, history and social studies, literature, science, fine arts, and mathematics (Pace 1979, 1984).

OUTCOMES ASSESSMENT EFFORTS: 1952–1975

The second period of outcomes assessment history at colleges and universities was from 1952–1975. This period is commonly known in higher education as the Golden Age. It saw an increase in enrollment of eighteen to twenty-four year olds triple from 13.8 percent to 40.5 percent (Resnick and Goulden, 1987). This increase is attributed to demographic factors such as the baby boom, and an increase in minority enrollment aided by the passage of the Civil Rights legislation of the 1960's. In addition to these demographic factors, the increased importance assigned to a college education by society in general also contributed to the increase in college enrollments. Also, Jencks and Riesman (1977) say that the upward trend in enrollment was aided by the GI Bill.

State and federal governments have greatly influenced the size of the university student bodies without requiring any change in standards of admission in two ways. First, state and federal governments have done so by promoting the completion of courses of study in secondary schools, which has, in turn, resulted in more young persons acquiring the qualifications for admission to universities. And second, adding the provision of grants or loans to pay for fees and maintenance and of grants for the construction of new buildings at universities and for the payment of the salaries of larger teaching staffs were added by government (Shils, 1983).

During this time period the structure of institutions changed as they grew larger and more complex. Large state universities became multiversities, and the number of community colleges increased sevenfold. Overall, the number of accredited colleges and universities grew from two thousand to more than three thousand during this period.

In the four-year colleges and universities the curriculum changed dramatically as indicated by the changing patterns of student majors:

The student majors in the liberal arts declined precipitously. The portion of students majoring in history, philosophy, math, social science, literature, foreign languages, and science dropped from 40 percent to 20 percent. The major gainer in student majors was business. Selected as a major by 23 percent of those receiving baccalaureate degrees at the end of this second period of expansion, business had almost doubled its share of undergraduate degrees in twenty years (Resnick and Goulden, 1987, p. 82).

In addition to these problems various university based assessment programs were instituted to aid in the determination of attainment of student knowledge.

University-Based Assessment Programs

Various movements of higher educational reform (such as nontraditional education, and the professionalization of teaching) of the early 1970's on colleges campuses spurred the use of assessment techniques on college campuses. Some of the early experimenters with student assessment were specialized programs—such as the returning adult student and teacher education.

Nontraditional education began to receive greater respectability during the late 1960's and early 1970's. This movement was characterized by adult participation in the college experience. The returning adult student was often required to develop a portfolio documenting their knowledge and competencies gained outside of college. This information was then used by admissions and counseling officers to award academic credit for outside learning (Edgerton, 1986).

The field of teacher education used assessment as a tool to aid in its recognition as a true profession. During this time period, the Holmes group and the Carnegie Forum had recently issued major reports, calling for the transformation of teaching into a full profession. The Carnegie Forum called for the creation of a national board to develop standards and procedures for entering the profession. The initial version developed by Lee Schulman and Gary Sykes of Stanford University required the candidates for teaching certificates to not only take written tests but also participate in two-and-one-half day assessment exercises—videotape samples of actual teaching (Edgerton, 1986). These programs were followed by student assessment as a method of full curriculum review at small colleges such as Alverno and Northeast Missouri State University.

Alverno College

Alverno College, a small private women's college in Milwaukee, was one of the early innovators of student assessment measures. With the help of AT&T beginning in 1973, Alverno College developed a multiple measure assessment center program designed to help determine whether or not students were acquiring abilities such as critical thinking, problem solving, communicating, and making value decisions from the existing curriculum (Edgerton, 1986). The assessment center concept as used at Alverno was devised by social science researchers and management from the business community and the military. Byham and Thronton (1986) define assessment centers as follows:

An assessment center is a comprehensive, standardized procedure in which multiple assessment techniques such as situational exercises and job simulations (i.e., business games, discussion groups, reports, and presentations) are used to evaluate individual employees for various purposes. A number of trained management evaluators, who are not in direct supervisory capacity over the participants, conduct the assessment and make recommendations regarding the management potential and development needs of the participants. The results of the assessment are communicated to higher management and can be used for personnel decisions such as promotions, transfers, and career planning. When the results are communicated to the participants, they form the basis for self-insight and development planning (p. 143).

The student assessment center at Alverno was designed to emphasize the intellectual and personal development of its students. According to Ewell (1985), Alverno's student assessment program is comprehensive and has as its objectives: (1) providing feedback to individual students for their own progress, and (2) ensuring that the curriculum is effectively meeting established educational goals. These goals are met by conducting standardized tests and tests of psychological and personal development (Ewell, 1985).

Throughout the four years of study at Alverno, the typical student will undergo more than 100 performance assessments (Hartle, 1985). Simulations that require a student to demonstrate one or more of eight core abilities: effective communications; analytical capability; problem solving ability; valuing in a decision-making context; effective social interaction; effectiveness in individual/environmental relationships; responsible involvement in the contemporary world; and aesthetic responsiveness. Within each of the eight general abilities the student must demonstrate competence at six levels of performance (Hartle, 1985; Harris, 1985). The accepted criteria of evaluation for abilities remains the same for all disciplines at the college. It is a multiple-judge approach that uses faculty, peers, community members, professionals, and others that act as assessors (Hartle, 1985). This assessment center approach to student assessment at Alverno has had remarkable success and serves as a model for other small liberal arts colleges.

Northeast Missouri State University

Northeast Missouri State University (NMSU), a regional comprehensive university formerly a public teachers' college, began assessing their students in 1971 as a result of problems associated with their change in mission (Ewell, 1985; McClain and Krueger, 1985). The original intent of the program was to test curricular effectiveness by comparing the results obtained by its students with national scores on standardized achievement tests—primarily the ACT Assessment, the ACT-COMP, the GRE, and professional school entrance tests. The assessment program was expanded in 1974 when the university implemented a multifaceted "value-added" approach to determine the degree of learning achieved by its students (Hartle, 1985). Value-added assessment programs are used to determine:

The assessed contribution of undergraduate education to the development of identified student abilities. Generally used to refer to pre- and post-testing of students to determine change. Occasionally, "value-added" models assess growth from entry to a convenient mid-point in the curriculum (e.g., end of the sophomore year) (Boyer and Ewell, 1988, p. 3).

This value-added model was driven by three primary goals:

1. the desire to know everything possible about the student,
2. the wish to demonstrate that the university made a positive difference in the student's life, and
3. the desire to demonstrate that students who graduated from the university were nationally competitive (McClain and Krueger, 1985, p. 37).

Since the inception of its student assessment program scores on standardized tests have improved markedly along with changes in the curriculum, and as a result NMSU is now attracting better students (Ewell, 1985).

Special Programs

In addition to numerous university based programs listed above several key figures became interested in the classification of educational objectives. Central among these key figures was Bloom and his emphasis on developing a taxonomy of educational objectives.

Bloom's Taxonomy of Educational Objectives

Bloom's taxonomy was intended to aid educators with communication, curriculum development, and evaluation and was developed with the aid of twenty-four individuals who met at the 1948 American Psychological Association convention. Bloom's taxonomy consists of a pyramidal hierarchy of six major categories of cognitive learning. These categories include knowledge, comprehension, application, analysis, synthesis, and evaluation. The categories extend from single mental processes on one end of the continuum to complex thinking and learning processes on the other end of the continuum. In addition to being arranged from the simple to the complex, the categories go from the concrete to the abstract. Furthermore, they are supposedly cumulative, in that the skills at one level require that the skills from the less complex levels have been mastered (Lenning, 1977).

According to Lenning (1977), Bloom's taxonomy influenced the development of several other taxonomies of educational objectives. These taxonomies included the 1961 Proclamation of the Educational Policies Commission of the National Education Association; The Gagne's Learning Model (mid-1960); and The Florida Taxonomy of Cognitive Behavior (1967).

The NCHEMS Inventory of Higher Education Outcomes Variables and Measures

NCHEMS's Inventory of Higher Education Outcomes Variables and Measures was developed by Micek and Wallhaus (1973) as a method of classifying higher education outcomes. Two goals for the inventory as identified by Micek and Wallhaus (1973) were: (1) to aid institutions of higher education with translating goals into measurable terms, and (2) to help institutions of higher education develop a list of priority outcomes. The inventory was divided into three main categories: student growth and development; development of new knowledge and art forms; and community development and service. Included in the inventory was a list of educational outcomes and suggested measures to be used to determine whether or not outcomes were being achieved (Gambino, 1979). In addition to special programs like NCHEMS's Inventory, several national achievement tests were also implemented during this time period.

National Achievement Tests

According to Pace (1979) a new era of achievement tests began in 1954 with the introduction of the Area Tests of the Graduate Record Examinations. This test differed from previous tests such as the Pennsylvania Study in one significant way: it evaluated the student's ability to read, understand, and interpret knowledge as opposed to evaluating specific fields of knowledge and the recall of information related to a given subject matter.

This new era of testing was beneficial to colleges and universities for two reasons. First, they emphasized the understanding and interpretation of information which is a more important and lasting outcome of a college education. And second, they were more widely applicable to a diversity of students and colleges. On the other hand, the tests did not directly measure the specific subject matter of individual college courses and thus were less valuable in measuring the "amount" of knowledge acquired from college courses.

Another section of the GRE was the Advanced Tests designed to assess knowledge of specific major fields. These tests were specifically aimed at college seniors who were applying for admission to graduate programs. In addition to these tests the College Level Examination Program was introduced in the 1960's primarily to give "students college credit for knowledge they might have acquired out of college" (Pace, 1979, p. 27). Another examination introduced during this time period was the College Level Examining Program (CLEP).

SUMMARY

As early as 1932, the University of Minnesota established the General College specifically aimed at young people who were not necessarily interested in the traditional liberal arts curriculum or the various professional school curricula. Since its inception the goal of Minnesota's General College was described as knowing "what we were getting for what we were doing" (Eckert, 1943).

The General College was followed in 1944 by the Basic College at Michigan State University. The Basic College purpose was to develop comprehensive examinations for courses in the newly revised college curriculum. The program separated grading from instruction and de-emphasized the importance of intangible student characteristics such as interests, attitudes, appreciations, beliefs, and values in the grading process. In addition to these university based programs, three special studies were conducted in an effort to understand students' educational attainment during their college years: the Pennsylvania Study (1928, 1930, 1932); the Cooperative Study in General Education (1939–1944); and the Cooperative Study of Evaluation in General Education (1950). And finally, national achievement tests were developed by agencies such as Graduate Records Office of the Carnegie Foundation, the Cooperative Test Service, and the Educational Testing Service.

REFERENCES

Boyer, C. M., & Ewell, P. T. (1988). *State-based approaches to assessment in undergraduate education: A glossary and selected references.* Denver: Education Commission of the States.

Byham, W. C. & Thornton III, G. C. (1986). Assessment Centers. In Ronald A Berk (Ed.), *Performance assessment: Methods and applications*. Baltimore: The Johns Hopkins University Press.

Dressel, P. T. (1949). *Comprehensive examinations in a program of general education*. East Lansing: Michigan State College Press.

Dressel, P. T., & Mayhew, L. B. (1954). *General education: Explorations in evaluation*. Washington, DC: American Council on Education.

Eckert, R. E. (1943). *Outcomes of general education: An appraisal of the general college program*. Minneapolis: The University of Minnesota Press.

Edgerton, R. (1986). An assessment of assessment. *Assessing the outcomes of higher education*. Proceedings of the ETS Invitational Conference. October 25, 1986.

Ewell, P. T. (1985). *Levers for change: The role of state government in improving the quality of postsecondary education*. Denver: Education Commission of the States.

Gambino, A. J. (1979). *Planning and control in higher education*. New York: National Association of Accountants.

Harris, J. (1985). Assessing outcomes in higher education. In Clifford Adelman (Ed.), *Assessment in American higher education: Issues and contexts*. Washington, DC: Office of Educational Research and Improvement. U.S. Department of Education.

Hartle, T. W. (1985). The growing interest in measuring the educational achievement of college students. In Clifford Adelman (Ed.), *Assessment in American higher education: Issues and contexts*. Washington, DC: Office of Educational Research and Improvement. U.S. Department of Education.

Jencks, C., & Riesman D. (1977). *The academic revolution*. Chicago: The University of Chicago Press.

Learned, W. S., & Wood, B. D. (1938). *The student and his knowledge: A report to the Carnegie Foundation on the results of the high school and college examinations of 1928, 1930, and 1932*. Bulletin No. 29. New York: Carnegie Foundation for the Advancement of Teaching.

Lenning, O. T. (1977). *Previous attempts to structure educational outcomes and outcomes related concepts: A compilation and review of the literature.* Boulder Colorado: National Center for Higher Education Management Systems.

Lenning, O. T. (1980). Assessment and evaluation. In U. Delworth and G.R. Hanson (Eds.), *Student services: A handbook for the profession.* San Francisco: Jossey-Bass.

Levine, A. (1981). *Handbook on undergraduate curriculum.* San Francisco: Jossey-Bass.

MacLean, M. S. (1943). Forward to R. E. Eckert's *Outcomes of general education.* Minneapolis: The University of Minnesota Press.

McClain, C. J., & Krueger, D. W. (1985). Using outcomes assessment: A case study in institutional change. In Peter Ewell (Ed.), *Assessing educational outcomes.* New Directions for Institutional Research, no. 47. San Francisco: Jossey-Bass.

Micek, S. S. & Wallhaus, R. A. (1973). *An introduction to the identification and uses of higher education outcome information.* T.R. 40. Boulder, Colorado: NCHEMS.

Pace, C. R. (1979). *Measuring the outcomes of college.* San Francisco: Jossey-Bass.

Pace, C. R. (1984). Historical perspectives on student outcomes: Assessment with implications for the future. *NASPA Journal,* 22(2), pp. 10–18.

Resnick, D., & Goulden, M. (1987). Assessment, curriculum and expansion in American higher education: A historical perspective. In Diane Halpern (Ed.), *Student outcomes assessment: What institutions stand to gain.* New Directions in Higher Education, no. 59, XV(3).

Shils, E. (1983). *The academic ethic.* Chicago: University of Chicago Press.

Tyler, R. W. (1947). Forward to the Executive Committee of the Cooperative Study in General Education's *Cooperation in General Education.* Washington, DC: American Council on Education.

Historical Review of Federal and State Initiatives for Student Outcomes Assessment: 1975–Present

INTRODUCTION

After years of focusing on the expanding enrollment of students in the higher education system, and the corresponding problems such as equal opportunity and student access, the emphasis for higher education has once again shifted to educational quality and student outcomes (Hartle, 1985). Stimulating this shift were several major reports dealing with the quality of undergraduate education. This chapter will first highlight these reports before discussing the third period of student outcomes assessment history (1975–present). More specifically, this chapter will (1) review the history of federal initiatives in higher education; (2) present excerpts of the Secretary of Education's Criteria for Recognition of Accrediting Agencies as they relate to student outcomes assessment; and (3) look at state initiatives in passing student assessment legislation.

Central among the reports that stimulated the assessment movement was the National Institute of Education's Study Group on the Conditions of Excellence in American Higher Education report *Involvement in Learning: Realizing the Potential of American Higher Education* (Study Group on the Condition of Excellence in American Higher Education, 1984), which gave good marks to higher education's accomplishments in terms of adapting to growth and change, but noted that there was room for improvement. This report asserted that despite significant success in adapting to growth and change, all was not well in American higher education. Reasons cited were: only half of those who enter college for a bachelor's degree eventually receive it; colleges and universities have become excessively vocational in their orientation; curricula have been fragmented; the ideal of integration of knowledge has been diminished, and few colleges examine the learning and growth of the students they graduate. Twenty-seven recommendations were given based on three conditions of excellence: student involvement, high expectation, and assessment and feedback. Among the report's twenty-seven recommendations were five recommendations for assessment and providing feedback to help improve the effectiveness with which students, faculty, and the institution carry out their work.

Additionally, the Association of American Colleges' 1985 report *Integrity in the College Curriculum: A Report to the Academic Community* released in February 1985 by the Association of American Colleges, reviewed the decline and devaluation of the undergraduate degree. It urged faculty to take responsibility for the curriculum at their institutions. The report suggested that a minimum required curriculum should consist of inquiry, abstract logical thinking, and critical analysis; literacy, writing, reading, speaking, and listening; understanding numerical data; historical consciousness; science; values; art; international and multicultural experiences; and study in depth.

Finally, the National Endowment for the Humanities' 1984 report *To Reclaim a Legacy: A Report on the Humanities in Higher Education* written by William Bennett in November 1984, sealed higher education's fate. Bennett's report claimed that colleges and universities were failing to give students an adequate education in the culture and civilization of which they are members (Boyer, 1985; Ewell, 1985). The report recommended that all colleges and universities should offer a "core of common studies" to include a chronological understanding of Western civilization; several masterworks of English, American, and European literature; proficiency in a foreign language; and familiarity with at least one non-Western culture. These reports along with dissatisfaction and mistrust of existing accountability measures being conducted by accreditation agencies and specialized program agencies fueled the spread of student assessment in the United States. In addition, Bennett turned his attention to the outcomes of higher education.

In November 1985, Bennett warned higher education through a speech before the American Council on Education that public colleges and universities in the United States should "state their goals, measure their success in meeting those goals, and make the results available to everyone." He also warned that, "If institutions don't assess their own performance, others—either state or commercial outfits—will most likely do it" (Staff, 1985, p. 25). In addition to Bennett's push for outcomes measurement at the American Council on Education, the federal government (through the work of Bennett as secretary of education) intervened with ground breaking amendments to the "Secretary's Criteria for Recognition of Accrediting Agencies." The amendments published in the *Federal Register* in 1987 and 1988 urged accrediting agencies to inquire about postsecondary assessment results.

FEDERAL INITIATIVES

The federal government has been directly and indirectly involved in higher education affairs in a significant way since the Morrill Land Grant Act of 1862. However, since 1944 this role has steadily increased as is indicated by the following events and legislation:

- 1944 Serviceman's Readjustment Act, The GI Bill of Rights.

- 1948 Public Law 550 extended the GI Bill of Rights to Korean War veterans.

- Brown v. Board of Education of Topeka (347 U.S. 483) made school desegregation mandatory.

- 1957 National Defense Education Act.

- 1963 Higher Education Facilities Act provided financial support for public and private colleges and universities in construction of dormitories and other buildings.

- 1963 Vocational Education Act provided for technical education, state plans, and area vocational schools.

- 1965 Higher Education Act, omnibus bill of financial aid to students and to institutions.

- 1970 National Labor Relations Board claimed jurisdiction over private nonprofit colleges and universities with respect to collective bargaining.

- 1972 The Education Amendments to the Higher Education Act of 1965 established the 1202 Commissions for Postsecondary Education (Miller, 1980, pp. 245–246).

It was not until 1987 that the federal government became involved with student outcomes assessment. The federal government acted to aid in the acceptance of assessment measures through a proposed change in the Secretary's Procedures and Criteria for Recognition of Accrediting Agencies published in the *Federal Register* on September 8, 1987. This action was taken after former Secretary of Education Bennett called on the National Advisory Committee on Accreditation and Institutional Eligibility (NACAIE) in January 1986 to determine whether revisions should be made to the Secretary's Criteria for Recognizing Accrediting Agencies. The existing criteria had been in use since 1974. As expected, the NACAIE suggested only moderate revisions to the criteria for recognizing accrediting agencies. Among these revisions was a suggestion for accrediting agencies to obtain information on evaluations of program and institutional outputs. However, what materialized in the proposed criteria in September 1987 was a completely new set of criteria as opposed to moderate revisions.

The secretary's new proposed criteria for changes in existing procedures and rules "would place greater emphasis upon the consistent assessment of documentable student achievements as a principal element in the accreditation process" (Federal Register, 1987). More specifically the new criteria required that each accrediting agency should compel its educational institutions and programs to clearly specify educational objectives and implement assessment measures to verify and document the extent to which students have achieved these objectives. Degrees or certificates are to be awarded only to students who have proven educational achievement through assessment techniques. Student assessment objectives, assessment measures, and assessment results are to be publicized. And finally, information obtained from the assessment process should be systematically used to improve student achievement.

After the secretary published this notice of proposed rule making for Part 602 in the *Federal Register* (52 FR 33908) on September 8, 1987, comments were received that resulted in significant changes in the final regulations. Most of the commenters indicated that they would not support the proposal as written. However, a number of commenters stated that the basic principles were supportable.

Objections to the proposal were: (1) it differed markedly from the 1986 recommendations adopted by the NACAIE regarding the assessment of educational outcomes; (2) the proposal had the effect of placing Department of Education requirements directly upon educational institutions, which is explicitly prohibited the secretary of education by law; (3) the proposal indicated that assessment of student achievement is the only educational evaluation technique that can be used to establish the reliability of an accrediting agency concerning assessment of educational quality; (4) several commenters indicated their fears that the proposal would "homogenize" education and prevent future evolution of valid assessment techniques; and finally (5) some commenters suggested the broadening of the concept from focusing on assessment of student achievement to focusing on educational effectiveness.

In response to these comments the proposal was rewritten and published in the *Federal Register* on July 1, 1988. The revisions, although essentially the same, provided more latitude on the part of the accrediting agencies. First, the wording and title was changed to indicate positive responses to commenters suggestions. Second, a new emphasis was placed on students admitted on the basis of "ability to benefit" from the educational experience offered by a program or institution. It was stipulated that appropriate methods, such as preadmissions testing or evaluation should be conducted to determine whether such students are capable of benefiting from the training or education offered by a program or institution. Both versions of the proposed criteria are included in the appendix.

Although the federal government has received increasing complaints in recent years for establishing and enforcing numerous guidelines on civil rights, sex discrimination, and equal employment opportunities, few complaints on documenting student outcomes or institutional effectiveness were registered. One possible reason for this was that most college and university officials felt that student outcomes assessment information was necessary for both internal and external purposes. In addition, accrediting agencies were already moving toward outcomes evaluation as a part of their review process. Nevertheless, student assessment requirements could be seen as just another attempt by the federal government to impose more constraints on institutions' autonomy, time, and money. However, the states also realized the importance of assessing educational outcomes and thus many have intervened with ground breaking legislation to support their positions.

STATES' INITIATIVES

Historically, government has left the process of reviewing the quality of college programs to the accrediting associations. As is noted by Trivett (1976), most states accept accreditation as evidence of sufficient quality to qualify an institution for state licensure. The federal government, in turn, recognizes state licensure and accreditation as preconditions for eligibility for federal funds. However, after the release of several national reports including *A Nation at Risk*, with its inflammatory language about the rising mediocrity in our nations elementary and high schools, the states turned their attention to the quality of the college experience and the role of accreditation in the accountability process.

Despite the fact of its historic centrality to perceptions about institutional quality, voluntary accreditation came under strong fire from the states (Marcus, Leone, and Goldberg, 1983). The states did not believe that voluntary accreditation, as it had been carried out historically, could be a major element in the state accountability process. States held this belief for two major reasons: lack of public reporting and control of the process by the institutions accredited (Floyd, 1982). Also recognized as a weakness of accrediting agencies were lack of rigor and standards in the review process, lack of serious self-criticism on the part of institutional participants, and a "back scratching" ethos. Trivett (1976, p. 59) reported that associations do not monitor or enforce standards of excellence, nor did they report which standards a college failed to meet.

Those responsible for allocating and administering public funds have taken these criticisms seriously. Over the past five years a growing number of states have required their public colleges and universities to undertake student assessment programs on their campuses. In addition, to show that the states are serious about assessment efforts, many have linked assessment results to budgetary rewards or other tangible rewards (Ewell and Boyer, 1988). As a result the status of voluntary accreditation as the guarantor of excellence in academe has been threatened.

An additional threat to accreditation as the guarantor of excellence in academe came in 1986 when the National Governors' Association's Task Force on College Quality decided to focus on how colleges and universities could demonstrate that student

learning was occurring (National Governor's Association, 1986).
In order to assure accountability the task force concluded that
"postsecondary institutions must assess student learning and
ability, program effectiveness, and institutional accomplishment
of mission" (National Governor's Association, 1986, p. 159).
The task force made six recommendations for accomplishing this
goal by the year 1991:

1. Governors, state legislatures, state coordinating boards, and institutional governing boards should clearly define the role and mission
   of each public higher education institution in their state. Governors
   also should encourage the governing boards of each independent
   college to clearly define their missions.

2. Governors, state legislatures, coordinating boards, governing boards,
   administrators, and faculties should re-emphasize—especially in
   universities that give high priority to research and graduate instruction—the fundamental importance of undergraduate instruction.

3. Each college and university should implement systematic programs
   that use multiple measures to assess undergraduate student learning.
   The information gained from assessment should be used to evaluate
   institutional and program quality. Information about institutional
   and program quality also should be made available to the public.

4. Governors, state legislatures, and statewide coordinating boards
   should adjust funding formulas for public colleges and universities
   to provide incentive for improving undergraduate student learning
   based upon the results of comprehensive assessment programs.
   Independent colleges and universities should be encouraged to do
   likewise.

5. Governors, state legislatures, coordinating boards, and governing
   boards should reaffirm their strong commitment to access to public
   higher education for students from all socioeconomic backgrounds.

6. The higher education accrediting community should require colleges and universities to collect and utilize information about
   undergraduate student outcomes. Demonstrated levels of student
   learning and performance should be consideration in granting
   institutional accreditation (National Governor's Association, 1986,
   pp. 160–163).

Education Commission of the States 1987 Survey

Prior to these recommendations, some states had already begun to address the issue of student assessment. In a fifty-state survey done by the Education Commission of the States (ECS) during January and February 1987, it was found that two-thirds of the states had initiated formal assessment procedures. Of the states not reporting formal statewide assessment procedures, a majority reported some assessment activity at the campus level (Boyer, Ewell, Finney and Mingle, 1987).

Boyer, Ewell, Finney, and Mingle (1987) provide a "mosaic" of states' student assessment initiatives based on the 1987 ECS survey. They identified six levels of state involvement in student assessment: mandated statewide testing programs; testing for teacher education; early intervention programs; encouraging institutional action; assessment within existing statewide mechanisms; and, statewide monitoring of other outcomes.

Mandated Statewide Testing

Some of the early initiators of mandated statewide testing programs were New Jersey, Georgia, Florida, and South Dakota. These early programs generally emphasized the use of mandated basic skills assessment for entering freshmen, rising junior examinations, and value-added approaches to assessment. In the state of Florida for example, the College Level Academic Skills Test (CLAST) has been administered since 1982. Students enrolled in Florida's public colleges cannot receive an associate degree or continue to the junior year without passing this test of reading, writing, and mathematical ability. In addition to CLAST, entering freshmen must take an evaluation of basic skills at entry. If students do not meet state standards they must enroll in remedial courses (Morante, 1986). Newer states that have mandated statewide testing programs such as Texas have followed a path similar to that of New Jersey in mandating basic skills assessment of reading, writing, and computation for entering freshmen.

Testing for Teacher Education

Testing for teacher education emerged as a distinct area of statewide initiatives because of public concerns about the quality of the elementary and secondary teaching force. The ECS survey found that nine states reported testing initiatives in place for teacher education; another three were pilot testing a similar program. Most states have focused on tests of basic skills as a condition for college admission; others have instituted a rising junior examination. The majority of the programs instituting rising junior examinations use commercially available tests such as the Pre-Professional Skills Test from the Educational Testing Service.

Early Intervention Programs

Early intervention programs seek to identify students' deficiencies in basic skills prior to college admission. The belief is that if deficiencies are identified and addressed early then quality students would "trickle up" to the college level. Ohio and Indiana are representative states that use this method of early assessment.

Encouraging Institutional Action

Encouraging institutional action is the preferred approach by the majority of states instituting student assessment policies. Approximately fifteen states, including Virginia, have taken this approach to assessment. Generally, these states have asked institutions to develop explicit assessment plans and to report to their state board the results of their assessment procedures.

Assessment Within Existing Statewide Mechanisms

Assessment within existing statewide planning, quality control, or accountability mechanisms has been the route for Alabama, Kansas, Rhode Island, Nevada, Colorado, Illinois, Kentucky, and

Arizona. For example in Alabama, institutions are required to report assessment initiatives and outcomes measurement as part of ongoing quality assurance reporting.

Statewide Monitoring of Other Outcomes

Statewide monitoring of other outcomes is the last assessment category identified by Boyer, Ewell, Finney, and Mingle (1987). Some states monitor such outcomes as student retention, satisfaction and job placement of college graduates, and economic and community development. Two states where this kind of program is being instituted are Maryland and North Carolina.

No two states' initiatives are alike. Their initiators range from legislators and executive officers to governing boards and state university systems officers (Ewell, 1987, p. 24). Some states follow the "Florida Plan" of direct legislative action. These states and their corresponding legislations are Colorado, Colorado's House Bill 1187; California, California's Assembly Concurrent Resolution 141; and Virginia, Virginia's Senate Joint Resolution 125. On the other hand, New Jersey and Maryland follow the "Tennessee Plan" a program sponsored by a coordinating or governing board without specific legislation (Heywood, 1977; Education Commissions of the States, 1986).

As noted above, postsecondary assessment initiatives differ from state to state. Some states such as Iowa and Idaho have no initiatives in this area, although individual colleges within their borders may be actively involved in assessment activities. At the other end of the spectrum, several states like Virginia, Florida, and Colorado have detailed mandates requiring colleges to participate in assessment activities.

Outcomes or student assessment is a relatively new phenomenon at the state level. In some states individual institutions such as Northeast Missouri State University (Missouri) and Alverno College (Wisconsin) have been conducting assessment efforts for a number of years and thus serve as a guide for other institutions within the state and to institutions outside the state as well.

However, for most states the process of student outcomes assessment is relatively new and in most cases confusing. Since the
ECS survey was conducted in 1987, John Bernardin of the
AACSB Task Force on Outcome Measurement (1990) has conducted additional research on the subject.

In January 1989 Bernardin conducted a study of the fifty states
to gain insight into the role of government in the trend toward
outcome measurement. Bernardin's purpose was to determine the
states' policies regarding the use of outcome measures in assessing the effectiveness of higher education.

Bernardin began with profiles of state policy which were based
on research by the American Association for Higher Education
and the ECS. The 1986 profiles were mailed to academic officers
and executive officers in each state. They were asked to review
their state's profile and revise it based on the current status of
policy and programs, and to indicate any legislative, task force,
commission, committee, or board activity. Representatives from
each state responded to Dr. Bernardin's request. The survey
results indicated considerable activity at the state level.

There was also an increasing interest in using outcome measures in the budget process of state institutions. Fifteen states used
some form of student outcome measure as a basis for evaluation
by a state agency. These states were: Arizona, Colorado, Connecticut, Hawaii, Idaho, Illinois, Indiana, Kansas, Missouri,
Nevada, New York, South Carolina, South Dakota, Tennessee,
and Utah.

In addition, thirteen states had pending legislation, task forces,
or commissions charged with the development of a policy regarding outcome measures. These states were California, Delaware,
Georgia, Kentucky, Louisiana, Maryland, Mississippi, New Jersey, Virginia, Washington, and Wisconsin.

Virtually all of this activity has been initiated in the last ten
years. Most states which commissioned task forces a few years
earlier ultimately instituted some form of outcome measurement
as a basis for program evaluation.

The most common procedure is that the state frames general guidelines on the submission of a required university report which provides a plan and an assessment of effectiveness. The university is responsible for recommending outcome measures compatible with its mission and objectives. Some states have fairly standardized procedures for the submission of detailed information on student outcomes. South Carolina, for example, requires that each university submit a report covering eighteen specific categories of outcome data.

Tennessee and Colorado have directly linked budgets to an assessment of university outcome measures. Three other states— Hawaii, Indiana, and Illinois—have made the recommendation but have yet to implement a budgetary process which includes an assessment of outcomes. However, one should note that any specific overview of what each state is doing in the name of assessment will probably be out of date within a short period of time, therefore, a sample of model states have been selected to show what is being done in the name of assessment. The states selected for review are Florida, Tennessee, and New Jersey (a detailed review of Virginia's student assessment efforts is included in the appendix).

Florida

Florida's efforts to assess student knowledge are primarily done using two examinations: CLAST (College Level Academic Skills Test) and the College Entry-Level Exam. CLAST was initiated by the legislature in 1979 and has been administered in the state of Florida since 1982. CLAST is essentially a rising junior achievement test that students must pass in order to receive an associate degree or to advance to upper division course work at a four-year institution (Morante, 1986). Its purpose is to assure that students have acquired the reading, writing, and computation skills expected of them by the time they complete their sophomore year (State of Florida Department of Education, 1984–1985).

Passing scores on the CLAST achievement test have been raised over the years. The following passing scores have been established by the State Board of Education:

	Reading	Writing	Computation	Essay
8/1/84–7/31/86	260	265	260	4
8/1/86–7/31/89	270	270	275	4
8/1/89 & thereafter	295	295	295	5

Strong opposition to this testing program in Florida has been expressed. Studies indicate that minority students have not performed well on the test. Projections have been made of a massive failure rate by minority students in the future unless present conditions change (Morante, 1986).

Some unintended consequences of Florida's CLAST and the College Entry-Level Exam have been identified by participants. They are increased attention to English/math, sharing of instructional materials among faculty, stronger coordination between high school faculty and college faculty in English and math, statewide conferences, and a legislative commitment to the early identification and assistance for at-risk students (Bernardin and Ulrich, 1990).

Tennessee

Since 1979 the state of Tennessee has had a performance-based funding program as an incentive for educational improvement at its public institutions of higher education. Public colleges and universities within the state are expected to clearly define their objectives and to establish assessment programs to demonstrate how well these objectives are being achieved. Initially, Tennessee's incentive budgeting program was voluntary, but in 1984 it became a requirement for all public institutions. As part of this effort, the ACT Comp examination (an instrument designed to test general education competencies) is required of all students. While no passing score is specified, the results are reported by institutions and are used to influence each institution's budget. In addition, the State Board of Regents, which includes all public two- and four-year institutions of higher education, began a statewide basic skills assessment program in 1985. In the first year all entering students who scored below sixteen on the ACT were required to take a statewide basic skills test in language and mathematics.

In addition to the above initiatives, the state of Tennessee has also implemented a statewide evaluation system of its colleges' remedial efforts. Focusing on outcomes indicators, the program will analyze data on such variables as passing rates, retention, credit ratio, pre- and post-testing, grade point averages, and graduation rates.

New Jersey

The state of New Jersey has two student assessment programs: The Basic Skills Assessment Program (BSAP) and the College Outcomes Evaluation Program (COEP). The BSAP was established by the Board of Higher Education in 1977 and has two purposes: to assess the basic skills proficiencies in reading, writing, and mathematics of students entering college in the state; and to evaluate the character and effectiveness of the remedial/developmental programs at each of New Jersey's thirty public colleges and universities. This is done primarily by having students take the New Jersey College Basic Skills Placement Test which consists of four multiple choice sections: reading comprehension, sentence sense, computation, and elementary algebra. Morante (1986) identifies two purposes for this test: to place students in appropriate beginning courses and to collect statewide data on the extent and level of entering student proficiencies.

The second purpose of the BSAP is the evaluation of New Jersey's thirty public institutions' efforts to aid skill-deficient students through remediation. Efforts have focused on outcomes and multiple indicators of effectiveness. Seven indicators were identified: passing rates in remedial courses; retention rates; pre-

and post-testing; performance in subsequent subject-related college courses; grade point average; credit ratio; and successful survival rate.

In addition to the BSAP, the New Jersey Board of Higher Education created the COEP in 1985 to study college outcomes at its thirty public colleges and universities. An advisory committee composed of students, faculty, administrators, and members of the business community, government, and nonprofit sector was set up to plan and implement the program. The advisory committee, composed of twenty-three members, was divided into four subcommittees to study the following tasks: (1) student learning; (2) student development/post-collegiate activities; (3) research, scholarship, and creative expression; and (4) community/society outcomes (Boyer and Ewell, 1988; Morante, 1986).

In October 1987 the advisory committee presented its final report to the New Jersey Board of Higher Education. This report recommended that each institution assess general intellectual skills as well as the assessment of the specific outcomes of its general education program, student learning in the major, student development, and students' personal development and satisfaction. Additionally, each institution should assess the outcomes of faculty research, scholarship, and creative expression; its success in providing access and meeting the human resource needs of its population; and its impact on the community that it serves.

SUMMARY

Despite vast differences across the fifty states to the call for assessment initiatives, role models for the various types of assessment procedures can be identified. Role model states were selected for specific review based on their ability to show the vast array of assessment initiatives that are being conducted in the name of student outcomes assessment. For example, the state of Florida successfully uses the rising junior examination in its efforts to measure the communication and computation skills which community college and state university faculty members expect of students completing the sophomore year in college. Tennessee successfully tied student assessment initiatives at its public colleges and universities to incentive funding in an effort to encourage compliance. And New Jersey is important because it provides a model for both the testing of basic skills of entering freshmen and the measuring of college outcomes.

All of these states had to grapple with important questions such as:

- How can institutional diversity be maintained given the differences in student demographics, program, and institutional missions?

- How can accountability measures be balanced with improvement in institutional quality?

- What should be the level of assessment—the student, faculty, program, or institutional level?

- If students are the focus of assessment efforts, which students should be assessed—entering freshmen, rising juniors, or exiting seniors?

- Should there be a single instrument for all students at all colleges and universities within the state or should each college be allowed to develop its own unique instruments?

These questions are just a sample of those that must be addressed by states or institutions that are interested in designing successful assessment programs. They are by no means exhaustive. Answers to the questions will be unique to each state and will depend upon factors such as the political environment, economic standing, and the historical response of state government to higher education issues. Therefore, it is important for each state to identify variables that will affect the successful implementation of a quality assessment program and then proceed with an assessment effort based upon its findings.

REFERENCES

Association of American Colleges. (1985). *Integrity in the college curriculum: A report to the academic community.* Washington, DC: Association of American Colleges.

Bennett, W. J. (1984). *To reclaim a legacy : A report on the humanities in higher education.* Washington, DC: National Endowment for the Humanities.

Bernardin, H. J. (1990). Outcomes measurement: A review of state policies toward outcome measurement in higher education. *The Academy of Management News,* 20(1), 3–4.

Bernardin, H. J., & Ulrich, D. (1990). The measurement of student outcomes: State level activities (draft). An update of a 1986 report by Joni E. Finney and Carol M. Boyer.

Boyer, C. M. (1985). *Five reports: Summary of the recommendations of recent commission reports on improving undergraduate education.* Education Commission of the States.

Boyer, C. M. & Ewell, P. T. (1988). *State-based case studies of assessment initiatives in undergraduate education: Chronology of critical points.* Denver: Education Commission of the States.

Boyer, C. M.; Ewell, P. T.; Finney, J. E.; & Mingle, J. R. (1987). Assessment and outcomes measurement: A view from the states. *AAHE Bulletin.*

Ewell, P. T. (1985). *Levers for change: The role of state government in improving the quality of postsecondary education.* Education Commission of the States.

Ewell, P. T. (1987). Assessment: Where are we? *Change,* 19(1), 23–28.

Ewell, P. T., & Boyer, C. M. (1988). Acting out state-mandated assessment. *Change,* 20(4), 41–47.

Federal Register, Department of Education. (1987). *34CFR Parts 602 and 603, Secretary's procedures and criteria for recognition of accrediting agencies; Notice of proposed rulemaking.* Washington, DC: Government Printing Office.

Federal Register, Department of Education. (1988). *34CFR Parts 602 and 603, Secretary's procedures and criteria for recognition of accrediting agencies; Final regulations.* Washington, DC: Government Printing Office.

Floyd, C. E. (1982). *State planning, budgeting, and accountability: Approaches for higher education.* AAHE-ERIC/Higher Education Research Report no. 6.

Hartle, T. W. (1985). The growing interest in measuring the educational achievement of college students. In Clifford Adelman's *Assessment in higher education.* Washington, DC: Office of Educational Research and Improvement. U.S. Department of Education.

Heywood, J. (1977). *Assessment in higher education.* New York: John Wiley and Son.

Marcus, L.; Leone, A. O. & Goldberg, E. D. (1983). *The path to excellence: Quality assurance in higher education.* AAHE-ERIC Higher Education Research Report no. 1.

Miller, R. I. (1980). *The assessment of college performance.* San Francisco: Jossey-Bass.

Morante, E. A. (1986). The state of the states in postsecondary assessment. *Postsecondary assessment report of a planning conference November 20, 1986.* Center for Education Statistics. Office of Educational Research and Improvement. U.S. Department of Education.

National Governors' Association. (1986). *Time for results: The governors' 1991 report on education.* Washington, DC: The National Governor's Association.

National Institute of Education. (1984). *Involvement in learning: Realizing the potential of American higher education.* Washington, DC: National Institute of Education.

Nichols, J. O. (1989). *Institutional effectiveness and outcomes assessment implementation on campus: A practitioners handbook.* New York: Agathon Press.

Staff. (1985). Bennett calls on colleges to assess their own performance, publish results. *Chronicle of Higher Education,* 25.

State of Florida Department of Education (1984–1985). *Questions & answers about college and academic skills test in community colleges and state universities.*

Trivett, D. A. (1976). *Accreditation and institutional eligibility.* ERIC/Higher Education Research Report no. 9.

4

Accrediting Agencies' Influence on the Development of Student Outcomes Assessment Procedures

INTRODUCTION

Accreditation is the simple process by which higher education institutions voluntarily police themselves. The process was developed around the early 1900's as a means to differentiate between a "college" and "secondary" schools (Harcleroad, 1980; Folger and Harris, 1989). Since its initial focus on institutional protection through defining a college, accreditation has added two more foci—institutional quality and outcomes assessment—in an effort to be more responsive to the needs of the institutions of higher education that it serves (Folger and Harris, 1989).

This chapter will briefly review the purposes of accreditation, the history of accrediting agencies and accreditation as they evolved in the United States. Included within this historical review will be a discussion of outcomes assessment and recent efforts by accrediting agencies to include outcomes assessment in their quality review process.

PURPOSES OF ACCREDITATION

Throughout the history of accreditation numerous purposes have been identified. Selden (1960) identified four purposes of accreditation: (1) to solve problems related to distinguishing between a college and a high school; (2) the maintenance of academic standards in institutions of higher education; (3) a stimulant for institutional self-improvement; and (4) a protective barrier between institutions of higher education and forces that are continually being exerted on these institutions from both internal and external sources. However, since then other purposes have been identified.

Harcleroad (1980) lists nine purposes of accreditation that have evolved throughout the history of accreditation. They are:

1. Certifying that an institution has met established standards;
2. Assisting prospective students in identifying acceptable institutions;
3. Assisting institutions in determining the acceptability of transfer credits;
4. Helping to identify institutions and programs for the investment of public and private funds;
5. Protecting an institution against harmful internal and external pressures;
6. Creating goals for self-improvement of weaker programs and stimulating a general raising of standards among educational institutions;
7. Involving the faculty and staff comprehensively in institutional evaluation and planning;
8. Establishing criteria for professional certification, licensure, and for upgrading courses offering such preparation; and
9. Providing one of several considerations used as a basis for determining eligibility for federal assistance (Harcleroad, 1980, p. 8).

The inability to distinguish any one set of purposes for accreditation is a reflection of the ever broadening role of accreditation as a force in insuring institutional quality in the United States over the years. Since Harcleroad's listing of purposes in 1980 at least one other role has been added—the determination of outcomes of the educational experience at colleges and universities.

Ten values of outcomes assessment were identified by Patricia Thrash of the North Central Association and were reported by Jordan (1989). They are:

1. it helps institutions be more aware of the consequences and impact of what they do;

2. it improves planning and resource allocations at all levels;

3. it is increasingly used by state governing boards and legislatures as part of mandated procedures for program review, approval, and funding of public institutions;

4. it provides more accurate information for consumers;

5. it is valuable to private institutions in building effective recruitment and retention programs in times of intense competition;

6. it demonstrates institutional success which increases effectiveness in obtaining grants and other funding;

7. it encourages institutional improvement for its own sake;

8. it assists in the recruitment of appropriate faculty;

9. it serves students by accurately indicating what they can expect;

10. it promotes institutional accountability (Jordan, 1989, pp. 90–91).

These values are incidental to the accrediting process and its stated purposes and evolved as accrediting agencies' responsibilities expanded throughout the history of voluntary accreditation in the United States.

HISTORY OF VOLUNTARY ACCREDITATION IN THE UNITED STATES

Currently in the United States, there are six regional accrediting agencies that are responsible for evaluating institutions of higher education within their geographical area. They are:

- The Middle Atlantic Association of Schools and Colleges founded in 1887;

- The New England Association of Schools and Colleges founded in 1885;

- The North Central Association of Colleges and Universities founded in 1895;

- The Northwest Association of Schools and Colleges founded in 1917;

- The Southern Association of Colleges and Schools founded in 1895;

- The Western Association of Colleges and Universities founded in 1926.

These six agencies along with national and numerous specialized accrediting bodies exist to aid in quality assurance at colleges and universities. However, as one looks back over the history of accrediting agencies one will see that this was not always the case.

Historically, accrediting agencies have had to serve three functions: (1) institutional protector in an effort to distinguish between a college and a high school; (2) insurer of higher education quality; and (3) determiner of outcomes of higher education. These roles evolved as a result of external demands for accountability primarily from members of the higher education community and others such as the federal government that had an interest in the quality of colleges and universities in the United States. Each role will be discussed as it unfolded in the history of accrediting agencies.

Role One: Institutional Protector

Accrediting agencies and their related activities began over a century ago in an effort to solve two problems: (1) those related to the admissions of high school graduates by diploma rather than examination; and (2) the maintenance of academic standards in "colleges" (Selden, 1960, p. 42). These problems originated from several sources: first, the rapid spread of colleges, universities, and high schools after the 1850's; second, the move away from the classical curriculum; third, the development of the elective system; fourth, the addition of new degrees; and fifth, the drive to push some remedial college courses back into the high schools. These changes made it hard to define a college. Many colleges found themselves providing remedial education as opposed to "higher learning," thus the need for some kind of accrediting agency to set standards for institutions of higher education (Harcleroad, 1980, p. 7). New regional accrediting associations began to develop working definitions of the term "college" as well as establishing what preparations students seeking college admissions should have.

Accreditation emerged as a national activity in August 1906, when representatives from the four existing regional associations and representatives from the College Entrance Examination Board met "to present a plan . . . for establishing, preserving, and interpreting in common terms the standards of admission to college, whatever the method or combination of the methods of admission, in order to accommodate migrating students and to secure just understanding and administration of standards" (Young, 1983, p. 2).

In 1909, the North Central Association became the first to establish standards for accrediting colleges. During this same period, two important accreditation events occurred. First, the North Central Association of Colleges and Secondary Schools, which started accrediting high schools in 1905, decided to accredit member colleges. However, it was 1912 before the North Central Association established the first set of twelve specific criteria for accreditation, and 1913 when they published the first list of fully accredited institutions (Harcleroad, 1980). The New England, Middle States, and the Southern regional associations followed the North Central's lead and also established accrediting standards and put them into operation.

In the 1930's, the North Central Association adopted a new standard for accreditation. This new principle was based on judging an institution in terms of its purpose and its total pattern as an institution. This new principle, later adopted by other associations, made it possible for accrediting to be adapted to the ever-widening spectrum of postsecondary education institutions such as normal schools, junior colleges, universities, and technical schools.

The second important development for accrediting agencies during this period was the beginning of specialized accreditation through professional associations. Technically, voluntary, nonprofit educational associations began with the American Medical Association in 1847. However, little control was exerted until after 1900 when the Association reorganized. This had become essential because of the low state of professional schools of all types, including medical. Other specialized accrediting associations that began during this period are the Association of American Law Schools (1900), the American Osteopathic Association (1897) with its Committee on Education in 1901, and the Society of American Foresters (1900) (Harcleroad, 1980). The American Medical Association established its Council on Medical Education in 1904, developed a rating system in 1906, and prepared the first classification of schools in 1907. These actions evolved into specialized accreditation and established patterns for other professional associations.

The federal government made efforts to stop the operation of degree mills by using laws against fraud and abuse of the postal service. The apparent need for state controls on degree mills led to another push during the 1930's toward state standards and state accrediting of colleges and universities. After numerous discussions and national conferences on the problem, the emphasis was left to voluntary accreditation and only the most flagrant degree mills were put out of business.

In the meantime, the voluntary associations consolidated their positions nationally. Between 1935–1948, all voluntary associations moved to some degree toward the new principle adopted by the North Central Association, basing accreditation of individual institutions on the institution's own objectives rather than on a single set of standardized criteria. This helped them later to adapt accrediting to a wide diversity of institutions.

Major changes took place in accreditation from 1948-1975. In 1948, the Association of American Universities stopped its listing of institutions, which for forty years had been the most important form of accreditation listing of the educational quality of institutions. With its prestigious list no longer available, the regional associations lists became much more important. Another consequence was a rapid increase in the number of specialized associations. Over seventeen widely known associations were established.

This first phase of accrediting history—defining a college—was characterized by regional accrediting associations refining their standards for membership and developing procedures for assessing educational quality on the basis of an institution's self-study and by an evaluation of the institution by a group of visiting peers (Young et al., 1983). Accreditation's roles were expanded when the emphasis on quality was added to its initial mission of defining a college.

Role Two: Quality of Accrediting Standards

Institutional Concerns

This phase was represented by an increase in the federal role at institutions of higher education. The primary purpose of federal intervention was to use "federal appropriations to encourage wider access and opportunity for postsecondary students as a way to achieve national goals" (Young et al., p. 237–238). In achieving this diverse goal several pieces of federal legislation were enacted—the GI bills, the National Defense and Education Act, and the Higher Education Act.

The GI bills of 1944 and 1952 looked to higher education as the primary means of helping veterans get established in a productive career. A major part of the 1944 GI Bill provided education benefits that could be used for almost any type of education from elementary school through graduate school. Institutions would be reimbursed by the Veterans Administration based on the number of veterans enrolled. There was little to no control over the selection of institutions. Many schools lacked both accreditation and effective state regulation through licensing. This scandal led to the revised GI Bill of 1952 (Young et al., 1983).

In the GI Bill of 1952, Congress turned to the states for help in determining eligible institutions for VA funds. The states in turn, turned to accrediting agencies for approval of programs. Thus accreditation was a tool to aid the federal government in the dispersal of funds (Young et al., 1983).

In 1958 Congress passed the National Defense Education Act (NDEA) as a reaction to the Sputnik challenge. This act called on institutions of higher education to develop broad strengths in science and defense areas. Again accreditation was used to aid the Office of Education in determining which institutions were eligible for funds.

During the 1960's Congress passed the Higher Education Act which was an effort to provide higher education opportunities to economically disadvantaged students regardless of their preparation for college-level work. In a response to this challenge regional accrediting associations broadened their membership to include the rapidly growing community college and vocational school sectors. The expansion of accrediting agencies' roles to include responding to federal needs in addition to defining a college served as a template for the addition of another sector—student's needs.

Student Concerns

With the great expansion of colleges and universities in the late 1950's, 1960's, and early 1970's as a result of increased enrollments and increased governmental funding came a parallel growth in the responsibilities for accrediting agencies. After this time period a growing problem exploded, when the number of students defaulting on federally guaranteed loans rose rapidly and when it was alleged that the accrediting system could be held partially responsible.

"For Thousands Accreditation Has Spelled Deception" proclaimed an article in the Washington Post on June 26, 1974. Some students proclaimed they were defaulting on the federal loans because the institution in which they had enrolled had failed to provide the educational program it had promised. In a number of cases, the students claimed, the school had lured them with the prospect of a federally insured loan, which it was able to do because, being accredited, it was eligible to participate in the program. However, once the students had signed over their borrowed funds to the school in the form of tuition, the institution had its money and did not care if the student paid off the loan—if they didn't the government would (Finn, 1978). This accusation spurred growing concerns over the quality of accreditation standards.

The problems for accrediting agencies continued to grow. The federal government, realizing that it needed a better way of policing the schools, both to look after the interests of students as consumers and to protect its own monies, looked for other mechanisms for accountability. Because of the large amounts of federal money involved, officials of the executive branch advised Congress to gradually intensify federal oversight of the operations of accrediting agencies. The only other alternative was to monitor all the schools and colleges that participated in federally funded programs, a course of action that would enlarge the domain of direct federal regulation and erode the academy's ability to regulate itself (Finn, 1978).

Role Three: Outcomes Assessment

The focus on outcomes assessment was developed early among professional accrediting agencies for the licensed professions such as doctors, lawyers, and teachers. These groups required licensing exams for entry into the profession. The exams were considered to be a "proximate and relevant outcome measure for professional training" (Folger and Harris, 1989). If a student could not pass the licensing examination after completing his or her degree requirements, it would be impossible for them to work in their chosen profession. However, the focus on outcomes

assessment came more recently to regional accrediting agencies
and can be traced to the formation of the Council on Postsecondary Accreditation (COPA).

In 1975, in order to be more influential and to respond to
expressed limitations of accrediting agencies, the Federation of
Regional Accrediting Commission and the National Commission
on Accrediting combined forces to form the Council on
Postsecondary Accreditation (COPA). According to the COPA
board, COPA has five major priorities:

1. dealing with the problems associated with proliferation and specialization in accreditation;
2. evaluating educational quality and measuring outcomes of education;
3. coping with the role of government (federal and state) in accreditation;
4. developing a national education-information program on accreditation; and
5. selecting, training, and evaluating volunteers in accreditation
   (Young, 1979, p. 139).

During the past fifteen years, COPA has made significant
progress in addressing its second priority: evaluating educational
quality and measuring educational outcomes of education. After
receiving funds from the W.K. Kellogg Foundation, COPA
conducted a national study on nontraditional education. Nontraditional education is defined by Levine (1981) as any process that
generally describes students (such as minorities, women, and
adults) and curricula (such as external degree programs and credit
for prior experience) which are not integral parts of the higher
education system. Also, nontraditional education tends to focus
more on students' needs as opposed to institutional needs.

COPA's study on nontraditional education, completed in 1978,
was entitled *The Council on Postsecondary Accreditation's Project to Develop Evaluative Criteria and Procedures for the Accreditation of Nontraditional Education*. In conducting the study,

a review of all the accrediting procedures of each accrediting body recognized by COPA was performed. Also an analysis of the program and accrediting experiences of sixty-two institutions was conducted. And a national survey of 1,500 educators was conducted (Andrews, 1983).

Andrews (1983) reports that the results of the national survey of 1,500 educators found that they strongly supported a shifting in accreditation orientation towards the assessment of educational outcomes. This conclusion was based on responses by participants to a section of the survey dealing with the future role of regional accreditation. According to participants' responses to this section of the survey, their main concern was that accrediting bodies should "focus more on educational outcomes and less on structure and process" (Andrews and others, 1978, p. 112). This resulted in COPA's recommendation that all institutions of higher education would benefit from a new focus of accreditation bodies on educational outcomes. The study concluded that accrediting bodies should concentrate their energies on educational outcomes and should use the same standards and criteria for both traditional and nontraditional education in the evaluation of all kinds of institutions and programs that they evaluate (Astin, Bowens, and Chambers, 1979). Following the findings of the COPA study on nontraditional education, each of the six regional accrediting agencies responded by reviewing their basic standards and procedures in assessing educational outcomes and institutional effectiveness. Of particular interest are the actions taken by the Southern Association of Colleges and Schools.

The Southern Association of Colleges and School (SACS) Commission on Colleges responded to the COPA project by conducting a three-year study. This study was designed to review and evaluate its entire accreditation process and standards. The purpose of the project was to develop an accreditation process that would deal in a comprehensive and uniform manner with postsecondary institutions. Within this project, SACS conducted an extensive survey of colleges within its region. The responses to one question on the survey are significant (Commission on Colleges, 1981, p. 42):

The method of education is partly represented by the relationship between means and outcomes. The accrediting process can emphasize primarily the *means* of education (faculty, library, facilities, and so on) or the *outcomes* of education (what the student learns and can do as a result of education). Traditionally, accrediting agencies have emphasized means more than outcomes. In the future, would you like to see the accrediting process emphasize:

Responses	Percentage
1. Means totally	2.35
2. Means much more than outcomes	18.37
3. Means somewhat more than outcomes	24.12
4. Means and outcomes equally	33.98
5. Outcomes somewhat more than means	11.09
6. Outcomes much more than means	6.57
7. Outcomes totally	.12

The project concluded that although emphasis should continue to be placed on inputs and educational processes, SACS should include an emphasis on outcomes (Commission on Colleges, 1981). This project of the Commission of Colleges of SACS was the first comprehensive effort by an accrediting agency to identify, define, and apply the outcomes concept to the accreditation process.

One might ask, what were other accrediting bodies doing in response to COPA's findings on nontraditional education and outcomes assessment? To answer this question, Patricia Thrash, currently the director of the Commission on Institutions of Higher Education of the North Central Association, conducted a survey of regional and selected national and specialized accrediting agencies in 1984 and 1986 to determine the extent of their emphasis on outcomes assessment in their evaluation process. She found that:

- Outcomes measurement or evaluation of institution and program effectiveness is an integral part of accrediting agency evaluations, as expressed in their criteria, documents, self-study institutes, and evaluator training programs.

- Accrediting commissions offer a mixed response to whether there is or ought to be a relationship between outcomes measurement and public accountability, and whether outcomes and accountability should be viewed as related to educational quality.

- Accrediting commission officials express caution about overly narrow definitions of outcomes and the misuse of instruments to measure competence; they support outcomes as one important aspect of documenting institutional effectiveness, but stress the interrelatedness of outcomes and other criteria that must be applied in making an accrediting judgement, such as purpose, resources, organization, programs, and promise of continuing effectiveness (Thrash, 1988, p. 17).

While other agencies were questioning the need for a formal statement on outcomes assessment, the Southern Association of Colleges and Schools was implementing new criteria to emphasize outcomes of the educational process.

In 1987 James T. Rogers, Executive Director of the Commission on Colleges of SACS, stated in the foreword of SACS *Resource Manual on Institutional Effectiveness*, "We believe strongly that it is both proper and educationally sound to require that an accredited institution state its goals, develop methods by which the achievement of these goals can be evaluated, and finally, demonstrate that the evaluative information received is utilized in the planning process" (1987, p. ii). This new emphasis on results is evident in SACS' 1987 *Resource Manual* which included a new section, Institutional Effectiveness, designed primarily to address concepts such as determination of purpose, establishment of goals, and evaluation of results.

In an effort to push all accrediting agencies in the direction of outcomes assessment, Secretary of Education William Bennett released for publication a "Notice of Proposed Rulemaking" in September 1987 (see chapter 3: Federal and State Initiatives for Student Assessment). The effort, although directed at accrediting agencies, sounded the alarm for institutions of higher education urging them to focus on outcomes, or student achievement, as a condition for accreditation (Manning, 1988). Although many individuals, representatives from the accrediting community, and higher education associations responded to this action, few changes were made in the legislation. Then in July 1988, the *Secretary's Procedures and Criteria for Recognition of Accrediting Agencies; Final Regulations* was passed; thereby allowing the secretary to determine if accrediting agencies were systematically obtaining and utilizing "substantial and accurate information on the educational effectiveness of postsecondary educational institutions or programs, especially as measured by student achievement . . ." (*Federal Register*, 1988).

SUMMARY

Student assessment or outcomes assessments' roots are deeply intertwined in the history of accrediting agencies in the United States. Although accrediting agencies were initially responsible for a somewhat simple task—defining a college—this role has expanded to include emphasis on guaranteeing quality assessments of minimal standards in two areas: institutions and students. Additionally, a rather new shifting of attention towards outcomes assessment has been added to accreditation responsibilities.

COPA conducted one of the earliest studies of outcomes assessment of student learning for nontraditional education programs. It found that educators strongly supported a shift in accreditation emphasis towards educational outcomes, as opposed to focusing almost entirely on educational means such as the number of books in the library or the number of faculty members holding a terminal degree. Their findings were so significant that many of the accrediting agencies such as SACS decided to further investigate the need for outcomes assessment at institutions within their area. They also found that educators were in support of including criteria that emphasized outcomes of the educational process.

Since this early emphasis on outcomes assessment, Patricia Thrash of the North Central Association conducted a study in 1984 and again in 1986 to determine the extent of inclusion of outcomes assessment processes by regional, and selected national and specialized accrediting bodies.

One final push for assessment of outcomes came from Secretary of Education, William Bennett. In 1988 Bennett issued final regulations giving the secretary the power to determine which agencies will be recognized by the federal government, thus affecting the ability of institutions accredited by the respective agencies to receive federal funding.

REFERENCES

Andrews, G. J. (1983). Adapting accreditation to new clients. In K.E. Young and others (Eds.), *Understanding accreditation.* San Francisco: Jossey-Bass.

Andrews, G. J., and others. (1978). *Assessing nontraditional education.* (4 vols.) Washington, DC: Council on Postsecondary Accreditation.

Astin, A. W.; Bowens, H. R.; & Chambers, C. M. (1979). *Evaluating educational quality: A Conference summary.* Washington, DC: Council on Postsecondary Accreditation.

Commission on Colleges. (1981). Report of the subcommittee to survey the state of the art of outcomes assessment in higher education. Atlanta, GA: Southern Association of Colleges and Schools.

Federal Register, Department of Education. (1987). *34CFR Parts 602 and 603, Secretary's procedures and criteria for recognition of accrediting agencies; Notice of proposed rulemaking.* Washington, DC: Government Printing Office.

Federal Register, Department of Education. (1988). *34CFR Parts 602 and 603, Secretary's procedures and criteria for recognition of accrediting agencies; Final regulations.* Washington, DC: Government Printing Office.

Finn, C. E. (1978). *Scholars, dollars, & bureaucrats.* Washington, DC: The Brookings Institution.

Folger, J. K., & Harris, J. W. (1989). *Assessment in accreditation.* Sponsored by a grant from the Fund for the Improvement of Postsecondary Education.

Harcleroad, F. F. (1980). *Accreditation: History, process and problems.* Washington, DC: American Association for Higher Education.

Jordan, T. E. (1989). *Measurement & evaluation in higher education.* Philadelphia: The Falmer Press.

Levine, A. (1981) *The undergraduate curriculum.* San Francisco: Jossey-Bass.

Manning, T. E. (1988). Are the secretary's intentions honorable? *Academe,* 74(4), 12–15.

Selden, W. K. (1960). *Accreditation: A struggle over standards in higher education.* New York: Harper and Bros.

Southern Association of Colleges and Schools. (1987). *Resource manual on institutional effectiveness.* Commission on Colleges.

Thrash, P. A. (1988). Educational outcomes in the accrediting process. *Change,* 74(4), 16–18.

Young, K. E. (1983). The changing scope of accreditation. In K.E. Young and others (Eds.), *Understanding accreditation.* San Francisco: Jossey-Bass.

Young, K. E. (1979). New pressures on accreditation, *Journal of higher education,* 50(2), 132–144.

II

DESIGN, IMPLEMENTATION, AND EVALUATION OF STUDENT OUTCOMES ASSESSMENT PROGRAMS

5

Guidelines for Designing and Implementing Student Outcomes Assessment Programs

INTRODUCTION

Student assessment should be a systematic, continuous process if it is to yield constructive information that can be used in decision-making activities. This chapter is written to help campus officials who are interested in developing and designing a student assessment program think about what they want to accomplish within the framework of their institutional missions and goals. Since every institution has unique mission statements, histories, traditions, and objectives it is necessary to acknowledge that what might work well at one institution might not work well at another. Therefore, according to Folger and Harris (1989) it is necessary to research prior assessment efforts, consult others, and plan the institution's assessment efforts carefully before instituting a program. With this in mind, this chapter will present a systematic approach to designing and implementing student assessment programs.

Ideally, the implementation plans should be developed in conjunction with the design plans, but in the event that this is not the case, assessment program coordinators should be aware of possible stages that the assessment program will progress through. Assessment and evaluation literature (Bridger, 1989;

Davis, 1989) provides a wide variety of procedures and stages that can be used to implement assessment or evaluation programs. From this literature the author has identified several general steps within each stage that should be included in a systematic approach to designing and implementing assessment programs. These steps are typically carried out under a variety of circumstances and are affected by such forces as political agents, accrediting bodies, and college faculty and administrators, just to name a few.

The systematic approach to assessment that is presented in this chapter is based on the "life cycle" approach (Daft, 1989) and can prepare assessment personnel to provide proactive, effective, and relevant responses to calls for efficient assessment programs. From this perspective, this chapter will first briefly review Daft's life cycle concept (as applied to business organizations) in an effort to increase understanding and identification of the implementation stages of student assessment programs at institutions of higher education.

LIFE CYCLE CONCEPT

A life cycle suggests that programs are born, grow old, and eventually die just as humans do. Within the organization's life, program structure, leadership styles, and administrative roles follow a predictable pattern through four stages: entrepreneurial; collectivity; formalization; and elaboration. These stages are sequential and tend to follow a predictable progression pattern as illustrated in Figure 5.1 (Daft, 1989). The life cycle model is designed to provide a systematic starting point and frame of reference for campus officials who are considering an assessment program, trying to analyze why one has failed, or attempting to revive an ailing one. The steps within each stage are not intended to be comprehensive in scope and should be adapted by colleges and universities on an individual basis. However, the stages can provide a logical process and a model checklist for any college or university. With Daft's model as a starting point, it is the author's contention that institutional assessment programs tend to

Figure 5.1
Stages of Assessment Life Cycle

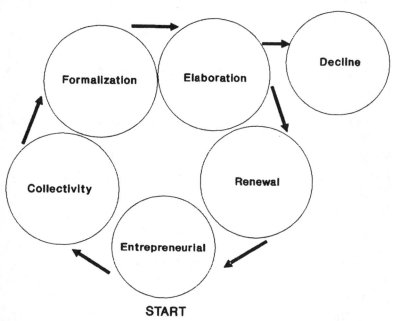

progress through the four cycle stages as identified by Daft (1989), but go beyond the elaboration stage to a fifth stage entitled "renewal or decline."

ENTREPRENEURIAL STAGE: IDENTIFYING PURPOSES AND AUDIENCES

The entrepreneurial stage is the first stage of a student assessment program's life cycle. In the entrepreneurial stage student assessment programs are conceptualized and developed by interested parties. These programs tend to be small, nonbureaucratic, and usually dominated by one person, the chief academic officer (CAO). The CAO generally provides the structure and control that is needed for the program to succeed. The CAO serves as a linking pin between the higher level officials at the university such as the president and the board of visitors (trustees) and the academic component of the institution (the faculty). Energy is devoted towards survival of the assessment initiative and the production of a single product—"highly educated students" who are results of the educational experience at the college or university. In this stage emphasis is placed on:

- identifying the need and intended uses of assessment program results;
- identifying key audiences and obtaining their support;
- shifting modes of thinking from input measures to output measures and;
- reexamining the institution's existing mission and developing a general mission for the student assessment program.

Identifying the need and intended uses of assessment program results. One must ask, Why are we proposing or undertaking an assessment initiative? Two responses might be because the state mandates assessment activities at its public colleges and universities, or for program and curriculum evaluation. The majority of responses to this question will fall into one of two categories— either for formative or summative purposes. Formative assessment procedures can be used to improve teaching, learning, and the curricula; to identify students' needs; or to assist the institution in the proper placement of students according to special needs. On the other hand, summative assessment data can be used administratively to allocate funds to institutional programs and to aid in other decision making areas. Summative or accountability assessment data can be obtained to satisfy accrediting, state, and federal requirements. Ewell (1987) warns assessment officials of the difficulty of serving both internal and external demands:

External demands for accountability constitute an a priori threat to an institution's choice of appropriate outcomes dimensions. First priority in assessment will inevitably be given to those areas perceived as important to general accountability, regardless of their correspondence to a given institution's purpose (Ewell, 1987, p. 9).

Either way, it is necessary for institutions to identify the purposes and incentives for assessment information prior to instituting a program. Bunda (1988) suggests that in order to satisfy both internal and external purposes, the assessment coordinator should finely focus program assessment so that results can be immediately applied to program redirection steps. In addition, program assessment should be focused broadly so that data will not change over a five-to-ten-year period. And finally, the data collection design and the final report should satisfy the need of the interested audience. Thus the challenge for institutions is to develop an assessment program that addresses both internal and external requirements with a minimum strain on existing resources.

According to El-Khawas (1989) the most popular uses or purposes of assessment information include:

Program and curriculum evaluation	78%
Reports to deans and department chairs	76%
Reports to faculty	73%
Reports to state agencies or boards	59%
Student feedback	58%
Accrediting review	50%

Understanding who uses assessment information is important to identifying who should participate in the assessment effort. It is also important to identify and include these actors early in the assessment effort.

Identifying key audiences and obtaining their support. In an effort to identify key audiences for assessment information an attempt must be made to answer the question: Who will make the decisions and evaluative judgments about the results of the assessment and the implications for change in programming or other areas? The answer might include internal individuals on college and university campuses or external parties. Regardless of who makes the actual decisions, the assessment process should involve the decision makers from beginning to end. This involvement should begin as early as the conceptualizing stage and continue throughout the planning, data collection, analysis, and dissemination of results stages (Forrest, 1981).

Internally, campus individuals from both the academic and administrative components should be included in the assessment process. From the academic component, obviously one of the first individuals to be included should be the CAO since he/she is primarily responsible for the success of most academic programs and changes. In addition, academic administrators such as deans and vice-presidents should also be included. And finally, support should be obtained from faculty, staff, and students who operate, serve in advisory positions, or serve in a decision making position within a program, many of whom have campus influence beyond their specialty area (Bunda, 1988).

From the administrative perspective, the key individual to be contacted is the Chief Executive Officer (CEO) who heads the administrative component of a university. Likewise, other administrative personnel such as those who work in student services who are interested in student performance and reaction to programs should be included (Bunda, 1988).

In addition to the internal academic and administrative personnel interested in student assessment, external groups are increasingly becoming more interested in assessment results. These external groups include state legislators who want to know what they are paying for, and accrediting agencies interested in reviewing self-studies of colleges and universities that they accredit.

Finally, the challenge for assessment personnel is to develop a program that addresses both internal and external requirements with a minimum strain on existing resources. As a general rule to meet this challenge, include anyone who will be involved in making decisions about the future of the assessment program or who will be directly affected by assessment results. One reason for this emphasis on involvement is that decision makers are most likely to have confidence and support in data that they or their peers and colleagues have helped to collect and analyze. Another reason is that decision makers are more comfortable with data they understand and thus can effectively communicate the results to others. This involvement is of critical importance to the success and continuation of assessment programs (Forrest, 1981). This will hopefully insure that assessment reports address each audience's needs.

Shifting modes of thinking from input measures to output measures. Traditionally, in higher education high quality has been judged primarily based on quantitative inputs such as the number of volumes in the library; how many faculty members possess terminal degrees; and how much money is allocated to a particular program. These input measures tend to be important in determining the status of an institution; however, they tell us little about the college or university in terms of its output or what actually occurs during a student's tenure in regards to the education process at the institution (Bergquist and Armstrong, 1986).

Output measures focus on student characteristics that they possess as they graduate from college. These characteristics include specific competencies such as critical thinking abilities, oral and written communication skills, and scores on standardized achievement tests such as the Graduate Record Examination. Bergquist and Armstrong (1986) warn that measures of output in isolation offer little knowledge of the true quality of programs offered at institutions of higher education. Additionally, the CAO must seek answers to the following questions that would aid in the determination of highly educated students. Are graduates of the college or university successful because of the program in which they were enrolled, or did they enter the institution already possessing the skills, knowledge, and contacts that they would later use to advance their own careers? Are the characteristics of graduates produced by the educational programs at this school, or did students at this institution acquire these characteristics before enrolling in the school or in other ways while enrolled such as through extracurricular activities? Answers to these questions will inevitably lead to a reexamination of the institution's missions and subgoals set within that mission.

Reexamining the institution's existing mission and developing a general mission for the student assessment program. Finally, one of the most important questions that should be answered at this stage is, What is our institution's mission, and how does student assessment fit within that mission? At this stage in the student assessment life cycle, it is important to let faculty, students, and administrators of the institution of higher education know that the institution is serious about student assessment. One way of achieving this goal is to alter the mission of the institution to include a conscious and deliberate statement on student assessment. This statement might read as follows:

It is the mission of this institution to improve undergraduate education by implementing ongoing and continuously evolving student assessment procedures that will support institutional effectiveness efforts in the areas of curricular development and renewal and administrative decision making.

The mission statement should serve as a guide to assessment plans as well as the operational activities of the college or university and would thus serve as a foundation for actions by representatives of the institution. By strategically placing a statement on student assessment within the mission statement, the commitment to student assessment will become well known and understood by individuals within the institution and by those external to the institution, such as legislators and parents of students who are interested in accountability measures. Modifications to the institution's mission statement serves as a catalyst to propelling the student assessment program into the next life cycle stage: collectivity.

COLLECTIVITY STAGE: ORGANIZING FOR EFFECTIVE ASSESSMENT

The second stage of student assessment programs' life cycle is the collectivity stage. In this stage, job assignments are made and a division of labor is established. However, the structure of the assessment effort is still mostly informal, although some plans and procedures are emerging. Faculty, staff, students, and others begin to identify with the goals of the program and with the mission of the institution. In general, members of the student assessment team begin to feel part of a collective. The following activities occur in this stage:

- appointing a program leader;
- positioning assessment program;
- setting up operating units for assessment activities.

Appointing a program leader. Strong proactive leadership should be obtained as the student assessment program begins to identify its goals and methods for achieving these goals. The new program leader must be responsible for providing clear direction and specific goals for the program, must have patience, credibility, and knowledge of institutional programs and traditions. Also, whoever is selected should be a good administrator and a proven manager. In selecting the leader, one should consider the fit between institutional needs and the characteristics of the applicants as opposed to comparing individual candidates to one another.

Nichols (1989) identifies three sources for assessment program leadership:

1. Academician—Some institutions find that the credibility gained by appointment of an "interested" member of the faculty to head implementation is worthwhile, given the sensitivity of the subject.

2. Institutional researcher—Given the primary quantitative nature of the assessment activity and the existence of an office with such expertise, a number of institutions have chosen to designate their institutional research officer to coordinate the implementation effort.

3. Institutional planner—Clearly the heart of institutional effectiveness is its relationship to campus planning efforts, and a number of institutions are choosing to emphasize the connection between institutional effectiveness and planning through appointment of a planning officer to coordinate the implementation effort (Nichols, 1989, p. 16).

In addition the assessment coordinator must have knowledge of assessment procedures, statistics, and sampling. Equally important, the coordinator must be able to organize and communicate effectively with a diverse population that includes students, faculty, and administrators at the college or university (Folger and Harris, 1989).

Positioning assessment program. Another point for consideration is the placement of the coordinator position within the organizational structure at an institution of higher education. Folger and Harris (1989) suggest that if the main purpose for student assessment is formative then the student assessment program should be placed in a staff position as opposed to a line position. One danger in that organizational position is that student assessment may be seen as unimportant and consequently run the risk of being ignored by the faculty it is designed to help. On the other hand, if the purpose of assessment is summative then it should be placed in a line position as part of the academic vice-president's office, for example. However, Harris and Folger (1989) warn that this location for student assessment programs will emphasize its judgmental or accountability role and thus may be too threatening for most faculty to use its services. Many institutions have found that the most effective location has been a staff office that serves the faculty. However, strong support and strategic planning is described as being necessary for the process to be effective.

Setting-up operating units for assessment activities. After areas to be assessed have been identified, subgroups should be set up to conduct activities within these areas. For example, the College of William and Mary in Virginia identified four areas where student outcomes can be measured:

* Assessment of the major
* Assessment of general education
* Assessment of attitudes and values
* Assessment of behavior after college.

As expected, four subcommittees of the student assessment steering committee were set up to handle operations such as test selection and implementation of pilot studies that will be conducted in the next life cycle stage of an assessment program—formalization.

FORMALIZATION STAGE

The third stage of a student assessment program's life cycle is the formalization stage. At this stage the student assessment program is entering midlife. It involves the development and use of bureaucratic coordination and control systems as a linkage between top management—the CAO and other higher administrative positions and lower level assessment units such as the individual departments and faculty.

The development of support groups, formalized procedures, and a clear division of labor is established during this stage. Emphasis is placed on technical requirements, structured procedures, and controls for the assessment program. This helps the student assessment program function without regards to political patronage or favoritism towards specific departments or disciplines that are participating in the assessment program. In addition, rules and policies help free top level officials from routine decisions; such matters can be delegated to subordinates that lead each group. It should be noted that the need for bureaucratization of methods and procedures is the primary drawback of the formalization stage.

One solution to a stale bureaucratic institutional program is the development of an organic student assessment program. An organic student assessment program relies on the adaptive capacities of individuals as opposed to formal structure. In an organic program continual adjustment of behaviors and roles designed to accomplish the program's goals is expected of participants as the nature of the assessment work changes, but there is no expectation that these roles be codified precisely in written job descriptions. Coordination of the student assessment program is expected to occur informally as various tasks demand, rather than according to a formal chain of command. Also, planning is not restricted to a top-downward process but flows up, down, and across institutional levels.

Organic student assessment programs are necessary in colleges and universities where primary employees are professionals. These employees have extensive knowledge and are generally able to work without close supervision or rules and regulations. To the extent the student assessment program leader encourages open expression of ideas and input from these individuals, the assessment program stands a better chance of success. The experience, training, and socialization of professionals thus act as a substitute for bureaucracy. Having identified some of the possible solutions to problems that occur in the formalization stage it is necessary to outline the activities that will occur in this stage. They are:

- Establishment of a time schedule for administration of assessment program;
- Identification of types of data to be collected;
- Selection or development of appropriate assessment instruments and;
- Collection and analysis of assessment data.

Establishment of a time schedule for administration of assessment program. It is important for the members working on the student assessment project to be aware of any time constraints that are imposed. For example, the state government might want a report on student assessment efforts by the next legislative period. Therefore, it would be necessary for institutions to organize and respond almost immediately. Assessment information would be useless if provided sometime after the expected deadline.

Miller (1988) states that the timetable must be flexible enough to respond to unforseen events and should serve as a general guide to assessment activities rather than as a prescription for action. Another time consideration occurs within the college or university; major assessment initiatives should not be conducted when other major activities are being enacted such as final examinations for the students.

Identification of types of data to be collected. Areas to be assessed depend largely on the mission of the institutions, charges from constituents, and more specifically on the stated goals of the assessment program. Areas that might be assessed are: (1) student majors; (2) general education; (3) attitudes and values; and (4) after-college experiences as identified in the collectivity stage. Within these areas or units for assessment many types of assessment outcomes can be identified. Ewell (1985) offers the following list:

- *Cognitive versus noncognitive outcomes.* Cognitive measures are those that are designed to identify gains in knowledge. On the other hand, noncognitive measures are those that are designed to determine changes in attitudes and values.

- *Psychological versus behavioral outcomes.* Psychological is described as internal changes in thinking that occur inside a student's head, whereas behavioral changes are changes in actions that can be observed externally.

- *Within-college versus after-college outcomes.* Outcomes that occur while the student is still enrolled in a college or university are labeled as within changes. This might include the change of major from biology to general business. On the other hand, those outcomes that occur after the student has graduated from college are labeled after-college outcomes. An example of after-college outcomes is the enrollment of the student in a graduate program.

Once the areas to be assessed and the purpose and objectives for conducting student assessment have been established the next step involves developing a response to the question of what type of assessment data to collect as part of the assessment program. The first and most immediate objective is to obtain valid information about institutional functioning. Collecting the right type of data should increase the likelihood that the information is honest, reliable, and complete. However, answers to the type of assessment data to be collected are oftentimes predetermined by internal as well as external accountability agents. This information might include data on students, educational and administrative personnel, curricula, programs, departments, and institutions. If for example emphasis is placed on students, the data might include information pertaining to:

- Student attitudes and values
- Student academic achievement
- Social development and awareness
- Personal development
- Career and vocational development

The Association of American College's (AAC) report *Integrity in the College Curriculum: A Report to the Academic Community* (1985) suggested a set of nine "essential experiences" for all undergraduate students. They are:

- Inquiry, abstract logical thinking, critical analysis
- Literacy: writing, reading, speaking, listening
- Understanding numerical data

- Historical consciousness
- Science
- Values
- Art
- International and multicultural experiences
- Study in depth

The AAC's list can serve as a template for guiding decisions on the "type" of data that can be gathered. However, it cannot be viewed as a "word for word" guide by every institution because of the individuality of campuses.

The Southern Association of Colleges and Schools' Commission on College requirements allows the individual institutions to decide what goals to emphasize and what assessment methods (either quantitative or qualitative or both) to use in order to evaluate obtainment of their selected goals (Folger and Harris, 1989). Since most institutions of higher education routinely maintain and report vast amounts of data about themselves, much information already exists that does not require the development or adoption of tests or surveys. Nichols (1989) identifies five sources of assessment activities that may already exist on most college campuses.

1. Entrance examinations
2. Standardized and locally prepared tests of graduate students
3. Licensure examinations
4. Departmental alumni follow-ups
5. Existing institutional data systems

In addition to these existing sources of assessment activities identified by Nichols, institutions are also required to submit reports to various federal and state agencies.

For many years institutions of higher education have regularly reported information to the federal government on who attends and who graduates, what programs are offered and what programs are completed, and the human and financial resources used in providing higher education services. The primary report containing this information is the Higher Education General Information Surveys (HEGIS). In addition, other reports have been requested by the Office of Civil Rights, the Office of Vocational and Adult Education, the Office of Postsecondary Education, and the Equal Employment Opportunity Commission. These reports contain a vast amount of information concerning students, faculty, and finances, and thus are a rich source of historical data for use in assessment activities.

One might become overwhelmed with the enormous amounts of data already available or that needs to be gathered by colleges and universities. However, Sharp (1989) warns that "the meaningfulness of data derives directly from their link to specific statements of intention that have been composed within the whole system of institutional effectiveness and assessment activities" (Sharp, 1989, p. 82). Therefore the usefulness of the assessment data to be collected depends upon having set clear goals so that the assessment process can be a focused inquiry. For example, in determining what type of assessment data to emphasize, Northeast Missouri State University (Ewell, 1987) set three general goals, with focused questions under each of the three, for the next five years, as follows:

- To graduate students at the baccalaureate level possessing considerable breadth of liberal learning.

- To graduate students who are nationally competitive in their major fields, and who demonstrate mastery of their disciplines's subject matter and proficiency with its distractive methods of enquiry.

- To graduate students who possess self-esteem, self-confidence, and readiness to accept the challenges of adult life, sufficient to meet the requirements of change and professional/career adaptation, and to contribute constructively and creatively to society.

These three general goals can be used to narrow the focus of the assessment effort by specifying what the institution hopes to achieve and consequently can narrow the type of assessment data to be collected and methods to use.

Selection or development of appropriate assessment instruments. One of the principle steps in developing an assessment program is the selection of the particular procedures and techniques or measures to be used. Actually this refers to any activity to be engaged in that can be systematically noted and interpreted within the general framework and rationale of the program in a way that will contribute significantly enough to justify its inclusion. There are quite a number of factors to be considered in deciding which measurement methods might meet this standard. Furthermore, the choice of such methods is by no means limited to assessment tools now in existence, but may well include tailor-made assessment procedures or modification of existing ones.

Almost certainly any assessment program includes a variety of tests, but many additional procedures may also contribute. Examples of some of these are the interview, questionnaires completed by students, alumni, faculty, and others, to name a few. Even in the narrow sense of paper-and-pencil tests, there are a plethora of possibilities to choose from among those now being used in colleges and universities. When the additional possibilities for developing assessment tools are added, however, the potential task of choosing a particular and reasonable number of assessment measures can become almost infinite in scope. However, institutions must determine if multiple measures will be used to collect data or if different methodologies will be used to avoid mono-method bias (Campbell and Stanley, 1979)?

Krotseng (1989) has noted that within a given field, multiple cognitive measures such as standardized tests, local examinations, oral examinations, portfolio analyses, and demonstrations yield a more thorough picture of effectiveness than any single instrument alone. Trenton State College, Alverno College, Northeast Missouri State University, and the University of Tennessee Knoxville are just several institutions currently combining multiple methods.

In any research area the reliability of the results depends in part on the various procedures used to collect the data and in part on the appropriateness of the particular measure(s) chosen. As in other research endeavors, the reliability of the assessment results can be improved by the use of multiple measures. Although the term "multiple measures" is generally interpreted to mean two or more different measures of the same effect, it can also mean repeating the same measure at different intervals or, more rarely, having more than one observer measure the same effect at a single point in time (Pratt, Reichard, and Rogers, 1989).

The number of methods to be employed or the number of times each measure needs to be repeated to establish trend data is a decision that should be made based on the goals and objectives of the assessment program.

Basically there are two sources for assessment instruments: commercially developed standardized tests or locally developed in-house tests. Commercial tests are those that are produced by agencies such as the Educational Testing Service and made available for a set price. For example, in the area of general education Pike (1989) lists five tests that were available before 1987. They are:

1. the ACT Assessment Program examinations,

2. the College-Level Examination Program (CLEP) General Examinations,

3. the College Outcome Measures Project (COMP) examination,

4. the Graduate Record Examination (GRE), and

5. the Scholastic Aptitude Test (SAT).

However, since 1987, four more tests of general education have been marketed:

6. the Academic Profile,
7. the College Basic Academic Subjects Examination (College BASE),
8. the Collegiate Assessment of Academic Proficiency (CAAP), and
9. the Education Assessment Series (EAS).

Thus there are at least nine commercially available tests in the area of general education to choose from. When selecting an instrument an institution should keep in mind the goals and objectives of the education program that is being assessed. Oftentimes an institution will find that none of the available commercial instruments fit their needs. When this is the case, another option is for the institution to develop their own measures of student outcomes.

Developing an in-house instrument requires expertise in testing and measurement and is a time consuming process. However, testing companies are available to assist in the effort. One institution that has been successful at developing in-house measures is the University of Tennessee Knoxville (UTK). At UTK more than 45 departments have developed outcomes measures (Pike, 1989).

Data collection and analysis. In some cases as identified above, existing data can be used for student assessment purposes; however, in most cases institutions will need to collect their own data. Two advantages are attributed to collecting one's own data. First, proper data collection can add credibility to assessment findings. And second, thoughtful data collection can save money.

Appropriate data collection requires the data to be collected in a way which does not distort findings. Oftentimes it is expensive to test every individual within a given area identified for assessment, thus it is necessary to obtain a sample that is representative of the group. One method for doing this is to test a random sample. When random samples are used one must take care to ensure that the samples are large enough and that the demographics of the students within that sample are representative of the total population of students from which it is drawn. How large depends on the size of the group being tested.

Once assessment data have been collected, an intelligent analysis of the information is necessary. This involves the selection of analytical models and an interpretation of the findings. This information should be used to guide decisions in the elaboration stage of student assessment.

ELABORATION STAGE: DISSEMINATION AND UTILIZATION OF RESULTS

The fourth stage of a student assessment program's life cycle is the elaboration stage. The elaboration stage emphasizes the need for the development of skills for confronting problems and working together as an assessment team. To achieve collaboration, assessment teams may be formed across departments and individual disciplines within the higher education institution. Formal bureaucratic systems have to be simplified further and partially replaced by committees and task forces with leaders of each area of emphasis, that is, general education, alumni studies, and individual disciplines. The following activities occur in this stage:

- dissemination of assessment results; and
- incorporation of assessment results in decision making activities (evaluation).

Dissemination of assessment results. Pratt, Reichard, and Rogers (1989) state that:

Based on the assessment of outcomes and objectives, reports for presentation to academic and administrative departments should be prepared. Mechanisms for providing feedback from the evaluation should include written documents, probably in the form of a report addressing each of the stated outcomes/objectives as well as tabular data . . . An objective of the assessment process might be to summarize the data for each outcome/objective on one page through either a table or graph with a short explanatory paragraph highlighting the major findings (p. 132).

All parties interested in the results of an assessment initiative should receive copies of the results in ways that they can understand.

Incorporation of assessment results in decision making activities (evaluation). After assessment results have been obtained and interpreted, administrators, faculty, government officials, students, and others interested parties should turn their attention to questions such as, How will these results affect instructional methods? How should we alter our present advising system in response to these changes? How should I change my study habits in an effort to be better prepared for my classes? To what extent will student assessment information affect current budgeting decisions? These are only a few of the questions that might be considered after assessment results have been generated. Specific questions will depend on the institution, its mission, and its unique circumstances for conducting student assessment initiatives.

After the student assessment program reaches maturity, in the elaboration stage, it may enter a period of temporary decline. A need for renewal may occur as a result of shifts away from the original purposes of the program or because the original goals have been successfully achieved.

RENEWAL/DECLINE STAGE

If a student assessment program is to be effective over the long run, it is necessary for both academic and administrative officials at a institution of higher education to resist the temptation to view assessment as a one-shot project (Wergin, 1989). Instead student assessment projects should undergo a process known as "institutionalization." Institutionalization occurs when assessment is incorporated into established institutional practices such as planning, budgeting, student development programming, and comprehensive academic program review (Banta, 1989). If the student assessment program is not successfully institutionalized into the everyday functions of a college or university chances are it will enter a period of rapid decline which will eventually lead to its death or termination. However, for those programs that are successfully institutionalized, the life cycle proceeds through the following steps:

- decentralize assessment program;
- streamline assessment staff; and
- evaluation of assessment effort.

Decentralize assessment program. One innovative response that could help revitalize a struggling program is a reexamination of its structure. Once the student assessment program has been firmly established on campus, there should be an effort to decentralize its responsibilities. Instead of placing responsibility for student assessment within the overall institutional program, student assessment responsibilities should be handed down to the individual schools, departments, and programs. This will allow for decentralization of authority, and departmental faculty would thus have considerably more autonomy to run their assessment efforts as they see fit. However, the institutional program should remain as a central coordinative body primarily responsible for the dissemination of information and the issuance of assessment guidelines as they become available.

Student assessment programs that fail to revitalize themselves may level off as mature programs, or they may go into gradual decline and eventually be terminated thus completing the life cycle of the program. This threat is common in departments that are not committed to student assessment. Therefore it is the role of the central assessment program to ensure that all departments and programs are actively participating in the assessment effort.

Streamline assessment staff. Once the assessment aspect of a college or university is completed for the time frame suggested it is necessary to streamline the assessment staff. In order to be fiscally responsible, the program should be conducted with a skeleton crew that is capable of continuing without unnecessary support personnel hired primarily to complete assessment tasks such as monitoring examination periods, or mailing of surveys, etc.

Evaluation of assessment effort. Sell (1989) states that assessment should go through a feedback process that will enable participants to make improvements in the assessment initiative. Advice, alternatives, and suggestions for change need to be included in the assessment process. Because of the important nature of assessment program evaluation, it will be elaborated on in chapter 6.

SUMMARY

The success of a student assessment programs's life cycle will depend upon the specific characteristics of each institution of higher education that implements an assessment program. These characteristics include: structure, control systems, goals, innovations, and the ability to change. The life cycle concept may be used by colleges and universities in understanding assessment programs and for aiding administrators involved in the day-to-day decision-making process. Administrators must respond to problems in a positive, proactive way in an effort to move the assessment program through its developmental stages: entrepreneurial; collectivity; formalization; and elaboration as summarized in Table 5.1. The movement throughout the stages of its life cycle must be fostered by a strong leader who is committed to the concept of student assessment, otherwise, the program will gradually diminish and eventually die completely.

As institutions of higher education struggle to change, respond to challenges and opportunities, and to answer questions about their effectiveness, the need for assessment programs on their campuses is warranted. With this quest for self-knowledge there will be a corresponding need for concrete directions in im-

Table 5.1
Stages of Student Assessment Implementation

ENTREPRENEURIAL

* Identifying Need and Intended Uses for Assessment Program Results
* Identifying Key Audiences and Obtaining Their Support
* Shifting Modes of Thinking from Input Measures to Output Measures
* Reexamining the Existing Institutional Mission and Developing a General Mission for the Student Assessment Program

COLLECTIVITY

* Appoint Program Leader
* Positioning Assessment Program
* Set-up Operating Units for Assessment Activities

FORMALIZATION

* Establishment of Time Schedule for Administration of Assessment Program
* Identifying Types of Data to be Collected
* Selection or Development of Appropriate Assessment Instruments
* Collection and Analysis of Assessment Data

ELABORATION

* Dissemination of Assessment Results
* Incorporation of Assessment Results in Decision Making Activities

RENEWAL/DECLINE

* Decentralize Assessment Program
* Streamline Assessment Staff
* Evaluation of Assessment Effort

plementing student assessment programs. The life cycle concept as proposed in this chapter offers a convenient guide for institutions that are committed to a continuous, long-term method for assessing student learning.

REFERENCES

Banta, T. W. (1989). Weaving assessment into the fabric of higher education. *Assessment Update*, 1(2), 3.

Bergquist, W. H., & Armstrong, J. L. (1986). *Planning effectively for educational quality*. San Francisco: Jossey-Bass.

Bridger, G. (1989). Attitudinal surveys in institutional effectiveness. In J. O. Nichols (Ed.), *Institutional effectiveness and outcomes assessment implementation on campus: A practitioner's handbook.* New York: Agathon Press.

Bunda, M. A. (1988). *Assessment and policy analysis in higher education.* A paper presented at the American Educational Research Association Annual Meeting, April, 1988. New Orleans.

Campbell, D. T., & Stanley, J. C. (1979). *Experimental and quasi-experimental designs for research.* Chicago: Rand McNally College Publishing Company.

Daft, R. L. (1989). *Organization theory.* New York: West Publishing Company.

Davis, B. G. (1989). Demystifying assessment: Learning from the field of evaluation. In Peter J. Gray (Ed.), *Achieving assessment goals using evaluation techniques.* New Directions for Higher Education, no. 67. San Francisco: Jossey-Bass.

El-Khawas, E. (1989). How are assessment results being used? *Assessment Update* 1(4), 1-2.

Ewell, P. T. (1985). Editor's Notes. In P.T. Ewell (Ed.), *Assessing educational outcomes.* New Directions for Institutional Research, no. 47. San Francisco: Jossey-Bass.

Ewell, P. T. (1987). *Assessment, accountability and improvement: managing the contradiction.* AAHE Assessment Forum.

Folger, J. K., & Harris, J. W. (1989) *Assessment in accreditation.* Sponsored by: A Grant from the Funds for the Improvement of Postsecondary Education.

Forrest, A. (1981). Outcome evaluation for revitalizing general education. In Jack Lindquist (Ed.), *Increasing the role of institutional research.* New Directions for Institutional Research, no. 32. San Francisco: Jossey-Bass.

Jordan, T. E. (1989). *Measurement and evaluation in higher education: Issues and illustrations.* New York: The Falmer Press.

Krotseng, M. (1989). Cognitive assessment instruments: Availability and utilization. In J. O. Nichols (Ed.), *Institutional effectiveness and outcomes assessment implementation on campus.* New York: Agathon Press.

Loacker, G. (1988). Faculty as a force to improve instruction through assessment. In J. H. McMillian (Ed.), *Assessing student's*

108   DESIGN, IMPLEMENTATION, AND EVALUATION

learning. New Directions for Teaching and Learning, no. 34. San Francisco: Jossey-Bass.

Miller, R. I. (1988). Using Change Strategies to Implement Assessment Programs. In T. W. Banta (Ed.), *Implementing Outcomes Assessment: Promise and Perils*. New Directions for Institutional Research, no. 59. San Francisco: Jossey-Bass.

Nichols, J. O. (1989). *Institutional effectiveness and outcomes assessment implementation on campus: A practitioner's handbook*. New York: Agathon Press.

Pike, G. R. (1989). Assessment measures. *Assessment Update*, 1(2), 8–9.

Pratt, L.; Reichard, D.; & Rogers, B. (1989). Designing the assessment process. In J. O. Nichols (Ed.), *Institutional effectiveness and outcomes assessment implementation on campus*. New York: Agathon Press.

Raoul, A. A. (1983). Establishing successful faculty evaluation and development programs. In A. Smith (Ed.), *Evaluating faculty and staff*. New Directions in Community Colleges, 41. San Francisco: Jossey-Bass.

Sell, G. R. (1989). Making assessment work: A synthesis and future directions. In Peter J. Gray (Ed.), *Achieving assessment goals using evaluation techniques*. New Directions for Higher Education, no. 67. San Francisco: Jossey-Bass.

Sharp, B. H. (1989). Assessment related information from institutional data systems. In J. O. Nichols (Ed.), *Institutional effectiveness and outcomes assessment implementation on campus*. New York: Agathon Press.

Wergin, J. (1989). Politics of assessment in the university. *Assessment Update*, 1(2), 5–7.

6

Conclusion: Evaluating the Effectiveness of Student Outcomes Assessment Initiatives

INTRODUCTION

Student assessment, in one form or another, has existed at institutions of higher education in the United States since the founding of Harvard University in 1650. However, over the past seventy or more years the debate over accountability for college and university outputs versus institutional autonomy has been waged. The end result being the emphasis by diverse institutions, special programs, and testing agencies on the development of detailed measures to study the outputs of education. Many of these measures or examinations that were developed are still valued to this day for their reliability and validity (Pace, 1984).

Once again, interest has shifted to the outputs of higher education. Individual states and institutions of higher education have responded by setting up student assessment programs that are expected to aid in the determination of institutional quality, effectiveness, and commitment to institutional improvement. This requires that student assessment programs produce reliable data that can ultimately be used in the decision-making process.

A basic contention throughout this book has been that many student assessment programs exist on college and university campuses today, but very little effort has been made to utilize findings from previous historical student assessment efforts or more recent information on program design, implementation, and evaluation into current assessment practices. Why is this true? First, student assessment programs are often a reactionary measure to external calls for accountability. Oftentimes, in an effort to comply with external mandates and deadlines, there has not been sufficient time to properly research and develop stable programs. Second, the ties between student assessment results and institutional effectiveness are not recognized by many decision makers on college and university campuses. This inhibits decision makers from making informed decisions in many areas ranging from goal setting to budgetary allocations. And third, many college and university personnel still view student assessment programs as a fad, therefore, serious efforts to institutionalize assessment programs have not materialized on many campuses.

The purpose of this book has been to aid colleges and universities in the successful institutionalization of assessment programs by reviewing historical assessment efforts since 1918. In addition, a life cycle approach to designing, implementing, and evaluating student assessment programs was presented to further aid in the successful institutionalization of student assessment programs on college and university campuses.

The introductory chapter began by defining commonly used terms such as "measurement," "assessment," and "evaluation." Of particular interest is the definition of assessment: "Any process of gathering concrete evidence about the impact and functioning of undergraduate education" (Boyer and Ewell, 1988, p. 1). From this rather broad definition of assessment, one can see that the impacts or outcomes of the educational experience along with the daily functions of undergraduate education are important to the assessment process. Also implied is that almost any process of gathering information on undergraduate education can be classified as assessment.

IMPORTANT STAGES OF STUDENT
ASSESSMENT PROGRAMS

Several factors that contributed to the rapid spread of student assessment programs on college and university campuses during the 1980's shaped the present course of student assessment. These factors are nonexhaustive and included perceived curricular weakness, trends in the work force, political accountability, elementary and secondary reform, and reactions to former Secretary of Education William J. Bennett's push to assess educational outcomes. These factors caused higher education officials to respond by developing student assessment programs that responded to these concerns. Of particular importance in developing student assessment programs are three stages: design, implementation, and evaluation. Special attention should be paid to the successful construction of an assessment program within each of these stages.

Regardless of the type of student assessment program that is being implemented on a college or university campus, a systematic approach to its development can be helpful. In an effort to approach student assessment systematically, the following stages are proposed: design, implementation, and evaluation.

Design and Implementation

In the design and implementation phases of a student assessment program attention should be focused on conducting a thorough review of other student assessment programs that were attempted prior to the one in question. In addition, a review of assessment history will aid assessment personnel in answering key questions such as, What are the purposes or incentives for assessment?, What type of assessment data will be collected as part of the assessment program?, and How will student assessment findings be disseminated? These questions are important to the actual design and implementation of assessment programs. In an effort to systematically answer these and other question that emerge during the assessment process a life cycle approach is proposed.

The life cycle concept can be used to order activities that must be completed to aid in the successful incorporation of student assessment programs into university functions. In chapter 5, five life cycle stages are outlined: entrepreneurial, collectivity, formalization, elaboration, and renewal or decline. These stages outline points that have been discussed throughout the book. Although all student assessment programs will not fit perfectly within each of the categories because of their unique circumstances, there are critical areas upon which the life cycle model is constructed.

The entrepreneurial stage of the life cycle model is concerned primarily with the successful introduction of the concept of student assessment to the college environment. It is dominated by one individual, usually the chief academic officer, who is responsible for the introduction and oftentimes the success or failure of all academic programs.

The collectivity stage is concerned with who should lead the new assessment program, who initiated the program, who is interested in the results, what areas are to be assessed, and the setting up of operational assessment units. The success or failure of a student assessment program oftentimes depends on the incorporation of interested and affected parties into the assessment process.

The formalization stage is essential to the development of formal procedures such as setting the time schedule for administering the assessment program, selection of appropriate assessment instruments, and collection and analysis of data. It is important to have these areas covered during the formalization stage so that the assessment program can proceed routinely without regards to political patronage or favoritism.

The elaboration stage stresses the dissemination and incorporation of assessment results into the decision making process at institutions of higher education. This stage is critical to establishing the link between student assessment data as a reflection of institutional quality at colleges and universities. Oftentimes the results of expended assessment resources are not used because recipients lack the knowledge required to successfully interpret the results. Therefore, one solution is to write assessment results in a manner that can be understood by all interested parties.

The renewal or decline stage is dependent heavily upon the use of assessment results in the elaboration stage. If a college or university does not successfully incorporate assessment findings into their decision-making process, the program is probably headed for a rapid decline. On the other hand, if assessment results are useful and can be used successfully to justify decisions, then the program will be renewed. The renewal or decline stage is characterized by a streamlining of assessment staff and a decentralized approach to assessment efforts. The final step in the renewal or decline stage is the evaluation of the assessment effort.

Evaluation

As student outcomes assessment programs command substantial portions of colleges and universities budgets, chief executive officers (CEOs) are showing increased awareness to the costs of conducting these programs. Many are finding that their programs are not as efficient as possible in providing maximum return of invested resources. Oftentimes the results that are generated are placed on a shelf as opposed to being actively incorporated into the university's decision making process. This should not be continued—if, indeed, the purpose for conducting student outcomes assessment is to determine institutional effectiveness in achieving the goals and mission of the institution.

The importance of student output measures to the planning and rational management of colleges and universities cannot continue to be undervalued. Decision makers must identify and in many instances strengthen the bond that exist between measures of student performance (within individual departments, programs, and schools) and overall indicators of institutional effectiveness.

Once this bond is firmly established, decisions about goals and resource allocations should be made based on the interpretation of student assessment data.

The final step in the student assessment process should be the actual evaluation of the effectiveness of the assessment effort. How an institution's student assessment program will be evaluated should be considered along with the very earliest planning and design of the program (Hawthorne, 1989; Lenning, 1980). This would insure that all the needed data is collected at the appropriate time prior to and during the implementation stage. However, with more and more states requiring some type of student assessment information, institutions of higher education are finding that student assessment programs are being implemented in a crisis-oriented fashion, thereby, causing the omittance of this critical step—program evaluation—in their initial plans.

A second inhibitor to the successful evaluation of student assessment programs is financial standing. Institutions of higher education are finding that they must tighten their financial belts at a time when more and more external audiences are increasingly questioning the quality of educational outputs and management techniques that exist on college campuses. One effort to conserve resources has been the cutting of corners on student assessment programs. Since the evaluation component is not viewed by many as being essential to the operation of the program, it is eliminated.

Evaluation has become a necessary activity for the sake of feedback for the improvement of the assessment process. Tracey (1968), states that improvement of any program can be effected by:

1. Objective and coordinated evaluation of every aspect of the operation.

2. The application of imagination and creative thinking by all personnel.

3. Deliberate collection of the observations, ideas, and thinking of all personnel.

4. Critical analysis and synthesis of findings, ideas, and alternatives.

5. Systematic, time-phased development and tryout of policies and procedures as well as identification of resources (people, equipment, materials, time, space, and money) needed to carry out plans (p. 14).

Student assessment programs should be evaluated, but the process should not end there. As a final step the evaluation of the student assessment program should include a follow-up plan for the improvement of subprograms within the overall student assessment program. In preparing the follow-up plan, the following suggestions may be helpful.

Once the evaluation has been conducted, action should be taken to implement some of the changes that are deemed necessary for the improvement of the student assessment effort. If no changes are made, this would mean that the resources used in the evaluation were essentially wasted. A second action that would be almost as disastrous would be to try and improve every area at once. This would cause chaos and an undue strain on available resources. A reasonable response would be to develop a time-phased plan for improving each subprogram of the student assessment program in accordance with the findings of the evaluation.

To make full use of the evaluation findings, everyone associated with the student assessment effort should be included and should become familiar with the final recommendations of the evaluation based on the data collected. This group of individuals should include students, faculty, staff, and governmental representatives, just to name a few. Once representatives from each of these groups are attained, emphasis should be placed on the careful studying of the findings and recommendations contained in the final evaluation plan, since these findings and recommendations are the basis for the improvement plan.

The committee and subcommittee structure as set up in the student assessment program's design and implementation stages should be used in the evaluation stage to develop and implement the follow-up improvement program. This would be beneficial because these individuals are intimately familiar with the strengths and weakness of the present system and thus are in the best position for suggesting changes to the design and implementation of the student assessment program.

In order to encourage an honest and accurate evaluation, each committee and subcommittee member should be urged to identify real problems associated with the assessment effort. The following questions as outlined by Tracey (1968) are important:

- What is the deficiency?
- Is it administrative?
- Is it lack of personnel with the required skills and abilities?
- Is it merely oversight?
- Are resources lacking?
- Who is responsible for improvement?
- What should be done?
- Why?
- Who should do it?
- When?
- How?
- How can success be determined?
- And who should be responsible (p. 28)?

Once answers to these questions are obtained, a priority listing should then be established for the improvement program. The identified deficiencies that are deemed critical to the provision of efficient and effective service should be placed first on the priority list. In other words, those items which if uncorrected will be most limiting to the student assessment effort should have the highest priority. Associated with this priority list should be an accurate estimate of resources needed and potential constraints to implementing the necessary changes. Some of the resources/constraints for student assessment program evaluation that must be considered include:

1. Funding: the dollars allotted to cover student assessment program evaluation planning and implementation.

2. Time: limits imposed in developing and executing the evaluation. Time limits may be thought of as a sequence of "milestones," such as completion of pre-test and post-test data collection (for example, testing knowledge or skill usually by paper and pencil), completion of data analysis, dissemination of results to appropriate audiences, etc.

3. Human resources: trained personnel such as statisticians, computer specialists, research methodologists, other faculty, staff, and administrators.

4. Organizational climate: the trust and openness of administrators, faculty, staff, students, and others in providing and receiving evaluative feedback information.

5. Availability of data: availability and quality of institutional information such as records of students, departments and institutional performance, reports, records; availability of students and others for providing new data through surveys, interviews and observation.

6. Details of the student assessment program evaluation action plan: objectives, time-table, procedures, participants, location; possible use of strategies which overlap student assessment evaluation strategies, such as Survey Feedback.

7. Audiences: kind and number of key players of the evaluation; information needs and interests.

8. Technical ability and feasibility: availability and feasibility of using standardized instruments, computerized analysis and storage of data; logistics in collecting and disseminating results; competencies and abilities of persons involved.

9. Ethical concerns: privacy considerations, student and institutional confidentiality, obtrusiveness, or harmful aspects of data collection and reporting.

To a large extent, these are interdependent factors to which those responsible for the evaluation of student assessment programs must attend during the design of the student assessment program plan.

Those responsible for planning a student assessment program should address the following questions to ensure adequate evaluation of program outcomes:

1. Does the evaluation design fit the objectives of the assessment program?
2. Does the design address important issues such as student, faculty, department, etc. needs and expectations and institutional culture (expectations about authority, how hard to work, etc.)?
3. Does the evaluation method meet standards discussed by the developers of the student assessment program?
4. Does the structure for the program provide a framework where emergent issues can be addressed? Can the design be modified to address key stakeholders' felt needs without sacrificing objectives?
5. Can the design be carried out in the time allotted?
6. Does the design provide a mix of evaluation activities that appeal to different data gathering methodologies?
7. Is the evaluation logically sequenced?
8. Is there redundancy in information gathered in the evaluation effort? Should there be?
9. Does the evaluation design allow for on-going development of an institutional climate conducive to continued student assessment efforts?

Finally it is important for a college or university to continue to do those things that are being done well in the assessment effort. Tracey (1968) points out that little net gain results from the program that stresses deficiencies and at the same time permits strengths to deteriorate. Additionally, overemphasis on improving weak areas, along with failure to recognize strengths is likely to subdue motivation and commitment to excellence that is essential to improving the student assessment program.

SUMMARY

Ironically, by the time this study appears in print, the relatively short history of student assessment is sure to have changed in many ways. Presently, many states are still considering whether or not to pass legislation requiring institutions of higher education to provide some type of assessment information. Additionally, those institutions that are already in the process of conducting student outcomes assessment will have moved to another stage in the assessment life cycle. Therefore, it is important for this manuscript to review and draw relevant information from the experiences of a wide variety of institutions to date in such a way as to provide assistance to those who seek to better understand the notion of student outcomes assessment. The sources of data available to assessment personnel include the preceding chapters, visits to other institutions presently conducting assessment efforts, correspondences and telephone conversations with a variety of individuals involved with student assessment, and an ever widening array of conference proceedings, newsletters, journal articles, and books.

As interest in student assessment initiatives continue to grow, many individuals will find themselves asking where do we go from here? The answer of course depends on many things, ranging from the goals of the institution to expected results of the student assessment initiative. Logically, the next step should be the assessment of individual program, schools, and finally the institution of higher education.

REFERENCES

Hawthorne E. M. (1989). *Evaluating employee training programs: A research-based guide for human resource managers*. New York: Quorum Books.

Lenning, O. T. (1980). Assessment in evaluation. In U. Delworth, G. R. Hanson, & Associates (Eds.), *Student services: A handbook for the profession*. San Francisco: Jossey-Bass.

Pace, C. R. (1984). Historical perspectives on student outcomes: Assessment with implications for the future. *NASPA Journal* 22(2), 10–18.

Tracey, W. R. (1968). *Evaluating training and development systems.* United States of America: American Management Association, Inc.

Appendix: Secretary of Education's Criteria and Case Examples of Student Assessment Outcomes Initiatives

Excerpt 1: Explanation of Changes from Existing Procedures and Rules

The following is an explanation of the changes that would be made in existing procedures and rules by the proposed regulations.

ASSESSMENT OF STUDENT ACHIEVEMENT

There recently has been much emphasis within the postsecondary educational community on the effective assessment of student achievement as the principal measure of educational quality. The Secretary is in full accord with this trend and wishes to encourage it. Therefore, these revised regulations, in §602.17 in Subpart B, would place greater emphasis upon the consistent assessment of documentable student achievements as a principal element in the accreditation process. This emphasis would follow from an original justification for accreditation as the guarantor of the validity and reliability of educational degrees and credentials, and is in line with what Congress intended when it provided that the Secretary's recognition would help to assure that accrediting agencies were reliable authorities as to the quality of education or training offered.

The Secretary expects that accrediting agencies will respond to this emphasis on institutional quality as measured by student achievement in a variety of appropriate ways. Among other things the Secretary expects accrediting agencies to maintain full and accurate records. The Secretary invites comments about whether the provisions of this NPRM best ensure that accreditation standards and decisions reflect demonstrable student achievement.

Section 602.17 Focus on assessment of student achievement

The Secretary determines whether an accrediting agency, in making its decisions, places substantial emphasis on the assessment of student achievement by educational institutions or programs, by requiring that each institution or program

(a) Clearly specifies educational objectives that are appropriate in light of the degrees or certificates it awards;

(b) Adopts and implements effective measures, such as testing, for the verifiable and consistent assessment and documentation of the extent to which students achieve the educational objectives described in paragraph (a) of this section;

(c) Confers degrees or certificates only on those students who have demonstrated educational achievement as assessed and documented through appropriate measures described in paragraph (b) of this section;

(d) Broadly and accurately publicizes, particularly in representations directed to prospective students, the objectives described in paragraph (a) of this section, the assessment measures described in paragraph (b) of this section, and the information obtained through those measures; and

(e) Systematically applies the information obtained through the measures described in paragraph (b) of this section toward steps to foster enhanced student achievement with respect to the degrees or certificates offered by the institution or program. (Authority: 20 U.S.C. 1058 et al.)

Excerpt 2: Section 602.17 Focus on educational effectiveness

The Secretary determines whether an accrediting agency, in making its accrediting decisions, systematically obtains and considers substantial and accurate information on the educational effectiveness of postsecondary educational institutions or programs, especially as measured by student achievement, by

(a) Determining whether an educational institution or program maintains clearly specified educational objectives consistent with its mission and appropriate in light of the degrees or certificates it awards;

(b) Verifying that satisfaction of certificate and degree requirements by all students admitted on the basis of ability to benefit, is reasonably documented, and conforms with commonly accepted standards for the particular certificates and degrees involved, and that institutions or programs confer degrees only on those students who have demonstrated educational achievement as assessed and documented through appropriate measures;

(c) Determining that institutions or programs document the educational achievements of their students, including students admitted on the basis of ability to benefit, in verifiable and consistent ways, such as evaluation of senior theses, reviews of student portfolios, general educational assessments (e.g. standardized test results, graduate or professional school test results, or graduate or professional school placements), job placement rates, licensing examination results, employer evaluations, and other recognized measures;

(d) Determining that institutions or programs admitting students on the basis of ability to benefit employ appropriate methods, such as preadmissions testing or evaluations, for determining that such students are in fact capable of benefiting from the training or education offered;

(e) Determining the extent to which institutions or programs broadly and accurately publicize, particularly in representations directed to prospective students, the objectives described in paragraph (a) of this section, the assessment measure described in paragraph (c) of this section, the information obtained through those measures, and the methods described in paragraph (d) of this section; and

(f) Determining the extent to which institutions or programs systematically apply the information obtained through the measures described in paragraph (c) of this section toward steps to foster enhanced student achievement with respect to the degrees or certificates offered by the institution or program. (Authority: 20 U.S.C. 1058 et al.)

CASE 1: STATE INITIATIVE—VIRGINIA'S CASE STUDY

The historical origins and development of Virginia's student assessment initiative can be traced through the State Council for Higher Education in Virginia (SCHEV) planning documents (*Virginia Plan for Higher Education*) that have been published every two years since 1974 (Sims, 1989). In its 1974 *Virginia Plan for Higher Education*, SCHEV set three goals for higher education in the state of Virginia:

1. To provide each citizen of the Commonwealth access to the form of higher education most appropriate to his interests and abilities (SCHEV, 1974, p. 12).
2. To maintain institutional excellence in teaching, research, and public service (SCHEV, 1974, p. 16).
3. To guarantee to the citizens of the Commonwealth the accountability of the total educational process (SCHEV, 1974, p. 19).

These three goals can be summarized as access, excellence, and accountability. Elaborating on the third goal of accountability, SCHEV made the following commitments:

1. To assure the most effective and efficient use of all resources provided to higher education.

2. To assure opportunities for both the intellectual and personal development of the individual student and to help prepare the individual for productive participation in society.

3. To ensure state-wide and institutional accountability through coordination and cooperation among all elements of the state's total higher education community and between higher education and all other levels of education (SCHEV, 1974, pp. 20–21).

Inherent in these commitments were the future foundations of Virginia student assessment policy: (1) accountability for state funds; and (2) accountability for the quality of the educational process for students who graduate from Virginia's higher education institutions. Since these original statements made in 1974, little reference was given to accountability and student quality in Virginia's higher education institutions until 1983.

In its 1983 *Plan*, SCHEV stated that "quality in undergraduate education must be once again the focal point. Parents, students, legislators, and employers have all shown their concern" (SCHEV, 1983, p. 28). In general, students and society have been concerned about quality, and the attainment of skills and performance factors; whereas the institutions of higher education have persisted in thinking about bodies of subject matter. Thus, from higher education's narrow perspective, discussion has been limited to the quality of students entering the system; whereas society has been interested in the outputs of the system (SCHEV 1983). In order to eliminate this discrepancy, SCHEV stated that higher education must be willing to define its expectations and to judge results in an attempt to be accountable to students, society, and higher education itself. In an attempt to alleviate fears associated with government involvement in higher education affairs, SCHEV stated that assessment measures would not endanger higher education's central and important principles of scholarship or academic freedom. Yet, as SCHEV was gradually preparing its institutions for the upcoming student assessment initiative, state legislators were already taking action.

Following the publication of the National Institute of Education's report *Involvement in Learning* in 1984 several legislators began to ask questions regarding the quality of Virginia's public colleges and universities. Having decided that some type of legislation was needed, they with the aid of a prominent constituent that was interested in seeing assessment efforts begun on college and university campuses quickly drafted a resolution (Senate Joint Resolution #125) that called for a legislative committee to investigate the quality of higher education in Virginia. SJR #125 requested the Senate Committee on Education and Health and the House Committee on Education to establish a joint subcommittee to study the quality of higher education in the Commonwealth. This joint subcommittee was to be composed of eight members, two from the membership of the Senate Committee on Education and Health to be appointed by the Senate Committee on Privileges and Elections, and three from the House Committee on Education to be appointed by the Speaker of the House. The Secretary of Education, the Chancellor of the Virginia Community College System, and the Director of Higher Education at SCHEV would also serve as ex officio members. The subcommittee was requested to review national reports on the quality of higher education and determine from their findings how high quality higher education would be continued in the Commonwealth. SJR #125 was put before the legislature on January 22, 1985. It was accepted and referred to the Committee on Rules for further evaluation and comments.

Having heard about the proposed legislation the director of SCHEV, Gordon Davies, seized the opportunity to serve as guide to the legislation. SCHEV immediately persuaded the legislators to withdraw their proposal and propose a study resolution that would be conducted by SCHEV instead. Realizing that the higher education experts were primarily concentrated in SCHEV, the sponsoring legislators openly welcomed their suggestions for getting the legislation passed. More importantly, the legislature gave SCHEV total responsibility for conducting a study on the need for student assessment in Virginia.

Meanwhile, in an effort to prepare its public colleges and universities for student assessment mandates, in its 1985 *Plan*, SCHEV stated that the goals for higher education in the state of Virginia identified in 1974 were still valid and substantial progress had been made towards achieving them. SCHEV concluded from efforts to attain these goals that Virginia higher education was now positioned in such a manner that it was time to make a major move forward into the front ranks among state systems in the nation. According to SCHEV, this was a good time to raise a new question for discussion among Virginia's leaders and to set an additional goal for higher education. The question for discussion among Virginia's leaders: What must be done to move Virginia colleges and universities from their position of relative strength, particularly in undergraduate education but also in some research areas, to the very forefront of American higher education? The new goal: to place Virginia's colleges and universities among the best systems of higher education in the nation.

In achieving this fourth goal, SCHEV identified ten actions that it felt would make Virginia higher education the best in the nation. The fifth of these actions suggests that "as a condition of full guideline funding, that each institution develop systematic, non-anecdotal methods for assessing student learning." The plan should not be the same for each institution, but should respond to the diversity of Virginia's colleges and universities.

In response to the study request of the final version of SJR #125, Gordon Davies directed his assistant director of academic programs to conduct a study on the measurement of student achievement and the assurance of quality in Virginia higher education. This study was conducted in 1985 and accepted by the Senate as Senate Document #14 during the 1986 session of the General Assembly. Six recommendations of the study were later accepted by the legislature in SJR #83 that was proposed by Representative Benjamin Lambert of Richmond. The six recommendations for measuring student achievement at Virginia's public colleges and universities were:

- *Recommendation 1*: That the academic relationship between secondary and higher education be strengthened

- *Recommendation 2*: That all state supported institutions of higher education establish procedures and programs to measure student achievement

- *Recommendation 3*: That institutions administer tests to determine the entry level skills of students whose past performance, as defined by high school grades or Scholastic Aptitude Test scores, indicated that they might have difficulty doing college level work; and that each institution identify a minimum threshold of achievement to qualify for college degree credit courses

- *Recommendation 4*: That institutions with students whose skills fall below the threshold established for college level work provide remedial education to maintain access while improving the quality of students' performance prior to full participation in degree credit courses

- *Recommendation 5*: That an advisory committee to the Council of Higher Education be established to develop guidelines for designing good assessment programs, to assist the institutions on request to develop the programs, and to advise the Council on progress in this area

- *Recommendation 6*: That universities submit annual reports of progress in developing their assessment programs and concrete, non-anecdotal and quantifiable information on student achievement to the Council of Higher Education (SCHEV Senate Doc. #14, 1986, pp. 16-17).

In addition to accepting the above recommendations SJR #83 requested that institutions and their boards of visitors "establish assessment programs to measure student achievement; and that the Council in cooperation with the state-supported colleges and universities, should establish guidelines for designing good assessment programs and report to the public results of institutional efforts to measure student achievement in its biennial revisions of *The Virginia Plan for Higher Education"* (SJR #83, 1986).

Using the study's recommendations as a guide, the legislature passed a resolution (SJR #83) mandating that Virginia's public colleges and universities develop plans for conducting student outcomes assessment. These plans were to be submitted to SCHEV for approval no later than June 30, 1987.

In the summer of 1986 David Potter, leader of Virginia's student assessment project, left SCHEV for a position at George Mason University. He was replaced by Margaret Miller. Miller's recruitment took most of the fall of 1986 and some institutions had begun to feel that the SCHEV was not serious about assessment because of the lack of communication from SCHEV during this period. However, in November 1986 the academic vice-presidents from the public colleges and universities which were already in the process of developing assessment plans came together with SCHEV's staff to establish guidelines for student assessment that respected both the complexity of the issue and the need to provide statewide coherence to the assessment plans to be presented by June 30, 1987. In January of 1987, SCHEV established a task force of institutional representatives to work with the staff of SCHEV to develop details of the official guidelines. Final copies of the guidelines were issued to institutions of higher education in April 1987. The final version offered ten guidelines that broadly reflected the tone of Senate Document #14, attempted to respect the diversity of Virginia's higher education institutions, and also attempted to achieve a minimal level of consistency across plans (Ewell and Boyer, 1989; Guidelines, 1987).

The guidelines set up four categories that institutions were to provide information on. They are: outcomes in the major and general education; basic skills proficiency; the effectiveness of remediation in verbal and quantitative skills; and alumni follow-up. Within each of these categories, Virginia's public institutions of higher education were expected to present concrete, non-anecdotal, and quantifiable results.

The executive branch of Virginia's government got involved with student assessment in May 1987. In Governor Gerald Baliles' guidance memorandum for the development of the 1988–1990 biennial budget requests that year, he stated that in order to receive "incentive funding" public institutions of higher education in the state of Virginia must submit an acceptable assessment plan to SCHEV by the June 30, 1987 deadline.

This action showed that the state government was serious about assessment. Now, SCHEV had both the legislative and executive branch's political and financial support in demanding institutional compliance with the student assessment policy.

In addition to political support, SCHEV responsibilities were expanded. Determining the acceptability of assessment plans was now an explicit SCHEV responsibility. This linking of compliance to incentive funding resources has been identified by Peter Ewell, student assessment expert, as the single most important decision taken by state authorities in Virginia's approach to assessment. Ewell reports that:

The decision to link assessment with state funding was critical and had a number of immediate consequences. Certainly it got the attention of the institutions by signalling the fact that the state authorities were serious about assessment . . . [O]ne SCHEV staff member noted, "we found that it was easier to get what we wanted with a kind word and a gun than with just a kind word." And this signal did indeed have the desired effect of forcing institutional closure on the issue: clearly under the circumstances it was less possible to do nothing or to report that assessment was "under discussion" by the faculty (Ewell and Boyer, 1989, p. 4)

In 1987 all of Virginia's public colleges and universities provided acceptable plans that were approved by SCHEV. As expected, each assessment plan was a reflection of diversity in mission, student population, and tradition at each institution. Several colleges such as George Mason University, James Madison University, and The College of William and Mary developed exemplary innovative plans.

In 1989, SCHEV's authority to oversee Virginia's student assessment initiative was expanded. Originally in the wording of SJR #125 and SJR 83 SCHEV's authority to oversee assessment compliance was merely a special assignment, however with the passage of Senate Bill #534 (SB #534) by the legislature SCHEV was given permanent responsibility for assessment. SB #534 amended the State Code of Virginia giving SCHEV formal authority to "develop in cooperation with institutions of higher education guidelines for the assessment of student learning." This action was viewed with hostility by some because it gave strong powers to an agency (SCHEV) that was originally setup to simply "coordinate" higher education in the state. To others it was welcomed because it virtually insured biannual base-budget funding for student assessment in the state.

Virginia's student assessment policy formulation process is important because it serves as an interesting example for other states that have not yet instituted student assessment legislation. By mandating student assessment and then allowing the diverse institutions to develop their own methods of assessment, Virginia's policy allows its public institutions of higher education to maintain a high level of campus autonomy, thereby reducing fears of government intrusion and control.

CASE 2: INSTITUTION INITIATIVE—THE COLLEGE OF WILLIAM AND MARY CASE STUDY

The College of William and Mary (W & M) in Williamsburg, Virginia is a selective liberal arts university chartered in 1693 by King William and Queen Mary of France. Numerous historical figures such as George Washington and Thomas Jefferson have graced its historic campus. Primarily residential, W & M enrolls over 6,000 full-time students; 70 percent are from Virginia. W & M's comprehensive student assessment program was developed as a result of state assessment mandates and guidelines issued in the mid-1980's. In addition to meeting state guidelines,

W & M views student assessment as a reflection of its commitment to self-examination and improvement as well as a method to judge the attainment of its mission.

In general, W & M's mission is the development of individual capabilities through liberal education. More specifically, W & M's mission statement summarizes the institutions's views on what should be contained in its curriculum:

the curriculum seeks to develop those abilities that characterize a liberally educated mind: literacy, a command of language and sound augmentation in speech and writing; mathematical and scientific methodology; understanding of foreign languages and cultures; knowledge of the historical roots of our contemporary world; appreciation of the creative arts as an ordering and expression of human perceptions; and the ability to recognize and examine the values which infuse thought and action (W & M, 1986, p. 9).

W & M's mission statement served as a guide for the development of comprehensive assessment efforts which are viewed as an integral part of its responsibility to ensure educational excellence and the efficient use of university resources.

Traditionally, W & M has taken a decentralized approach to student assessment. The university's faculty have been given assessment authority to set and maintain academic standards for degree granting programs at the university. Thus the faculty within each school and department is in principle accountable for setting and maintaining academic standards. This responsibility has resulted in regular investigations of programs, faculty, and students over the years. These assessment efforts have been motivated by both external and internal demands.

At the institutional level, the university completed a self-study in 1984 which is a clear reflection of the institution's commitment to critical self-examination. The following components of W & M's mission statement are assessed in the 1984 self-study report:

- Literacy
- Mathematical and scientific methodology
- Understanding of foreign languages and cultures
- Knowledge of the historical roots of our contemporary world
- Appreciation of creative arts
- Recognizing and examining cultural values

This self-study was used as a framework for the development and implementation of the present state-mandated student assessment plan.

W & M's assessment plan as mandated by formal legislation (SJR #125) is guided by several principles:

- The College is committed to self-examination and improvement
- The assessment program will be sensitive to the unique aspect of W & M
- Student outcomes assessment is part of a larger process of examining institutional effectiveness
- Assessment data will be used as a guide to, rather than a substitute for, judgement
- Assessment is an ongoing and continuously evolving activity

Within this framework the design for W & M's assessment program was laid out.

Program Design

W & M's undergraduate assessment program is concentrated around individual departments within the institution. Within these departments, the faculty of each undergraduate concentration has been given power to develop an assessment program consistent with its goals and objectives. Each department is then expected to determine student growth in their major, general education, attitudes and values, and behavior after college.

Implementation of Student Assessment Plan

Organizationally, W & M's student assessment program falls under the guidance of the chief academic officer's (CAO) office. Within the program, W & M has appointed a fifteen person collegewide steering committee made up of faculty, administrators, and students. This committee appointed for a three year term is responsible for:

- Overseeing the implementation of the student assessment plan.
- Providing a link between assessment staff and the schools and departments within the college.
- Developing guidelines to assist departments in their self-studies.
- Establishing the elements of the institutional and departmental data bases.
- Providing information and assistance to faculty, departments, and administrators to develop and revise assessment designs.
- Communicate the plan and its stages of implementation to major internal and external constituencies, encouraging dialogue with these groups.

The steering committee is subdivided into four subcommittees that correspond to the areas of assessment interest: the major; general education; attitudes and values; and behavior after college.

W & M's assessment plan includes three implementation stages:

Stage 1 (1987–1988): Planning for Implementation. Planning the many aspects of the four major components to assess undergraduate liberal education will take place in this phase. Additionally, revised graduating senior and alumni surveys will be administered. The CIRP and DCSEQ surveys will be readministered. And scoring for the holistic portfolio analyses begins.

Stage 2 (1988-1989):   Pilot Studies. The department of Chemistry, Sociology, Philosophy, Accounting, and Undergraduate Teacher Education conducts pilot program reviews. Additionally the implementation of the General Education evaluation pilot studies begins during this stage.

Stage 3 (1989-1992):   Full Implementation of the Assessment Plan. All aspects of the assessment plan will be in place by this phase. Departmental reviews will be on-going; the approaches used to measure general education attitudes and values and behavior after college will be in place. All questionnaires, surveys, and interviews will be conducted and results analyzed.

Assessment of the Assessment Program

An ongoing review and evaluation of the assessment effort will be conducted throughout the three phases described above. This assessment of the assessment will be conducted by the steering committee and by a national assessment expert. Assessment/evaluation of the assessment program is intended to serve as a capstone to W & M's assessment activities. Information from this evaluation is to be funneled back into the assessment process in an effort to improve functioning.

CASE 3: PROGRAM INITIATIVE—AN EXAMINATION OF OUTCOME MEASUREMENT IN HIGHER EDUCATION: A BUSINESS SCHOOL PERSPECTIVE

Recently there has been a strong social and political push to incorporate outcome measurement into higher education. Outcome measures have been mandated by many state legislatures and by numerous accreditation bodies. Outcome measures include tests, exercises, surveys, and other instruments designed to evaluate the results of the education process. While outcome measures are not typically used in most business schools, their frequency will probably increase at a dramatic rate. Essentially, three options seem available to business schools at the present time regarding this trend: they can hope that the trend will decline; they can let the direction of outcome measurement be determined by others; or they can accept outcome measurement as a potentially useful educational tool and try to guide the form it takes in business schools (Albanese and Dobbins, 1989). Presented below is a brief overview of the American Assembly of Collegiate Schools of Business' (AACSB) development of a task force on outcome measurement to address the call for outcome measures, the major approaches currently used to assess outcomes in general education and in business schools, and some limitations of outcomes measures in business schools.

Task Force on Outcome Measurement

At the December 1987 meeting, the Board of Governors approved the establishment of an All-Academy Task Force on Outcome Measurement for a three-year period beginning January 1988 and also approved the following definition of outcome measurement: "is concerned with end-of-program assessment of the cognitive and skill learning that occurs as a result of the formal educational process in colleges and universities." The AACSB's project—the Outcome Measurement Project (OMP)—goal is to explore the use of outcome measurement in collegiate business education and to contribute to the debate on outcome measurement. The following (tentative) objectives were established for the task force (The Academy of Management, 1988):

1. To monitor and assess the objectives, activities, and programmatic thrusts of the AACSB in the area of outcome measurement.
2. To monitor and assess the proposed instruments, measures, and systems proposed to schools of business (especially within the management domain) for evaluating outcomes.

3. To make recommendations to the Board of Governors pertaining to possible actions and policies for the Academy in the domain of outcome measurement.

4. To serve as the formal liaison with the AACSB for the Academy in relation to outcome measurement activities and thrusts.

5. To communicate to the Academy membership through the Academy *Newsletter* on development, issues, and concerns in the domain of outcome measurement.

6. To facilitate and establish linkages with other professional associations relevant to collegiate business and management education in the domain of outcome measurement.

7. To make recommendations to the Board of Governors as to appropriate cooperative actions and policies of the Academy in relation to other major professional associations in the domain of outcome measurement.

The task force held its first meeting at the Academy's annual meeting in August 1988 in Anaheim, California. The meeting consisted mainly of an exchange of information and opinions members had about outcome measurement and a discussion of objectives and tasks (Albanese, 1988).

The First Task Force Meeting

One objective of the task force is to monitor and assess AACSB actions in the area of outcome measurement. During the first meeting one task force member reported results of a survey of a sample of members of the Academy's Personnel and Human Resources Division (Albanese, 1988). The objective of the survey was to obtain responses to questions about the OMP and outcome measurement. The survey results (based on responses from seventy-five Academy members) indicated fairly low familiarity with the OMP but a high degree of support for the use of outcome measures as a way of assessing academic programs.

Another member commented on outcome measurement from the perspective of the AACSB-sponsored study, *Management*

Education and Development: Drift or Thrust into the 21st Century. With few exceptions, he found little interest or action in business schools in implementing new outcome measurement activities. He observed that business school deans were experiencing little outside pressure to implement outcome measurement and expected that leadership in outcome measurement is most likely to come from outside the schools.

Two members reported on their experiences with programs directly or indirectly concerned with the outcome measurement issue. Features of Ohio University's MBA program were described. The program includes a year-long course in management competency (skill) development, a required internship, and some elements of outcome measurement. Another member discussed a system of operating in Tennessee in which universities can earn up to a 5 percent "budget bonus" from the state government for meeting various predetermined outcome measurement criteria (Albanese, 1988).

Several members offered comments prompted by discussion of the above items. One noted that there is a "level of analysis" issue in outcome measurement: the object of outcome measurement can be the individual student, the college or school, and/or the university. Another suggested there is a need to gather more information from Academy members about their opinions and beliefs about outcome measurement. Another member asked whether, after examining outcome measurement, it is within the province of the task force to recommend against an increase in use of outcome measurement. While not arguing against further research, one member cautioned that the task force should not "reinvent the wheel" in researching outcome measurement. Finally, another member commented that the task force should be proactive on outcome measurement, not just reactive to AACSB actions.

The task force discussed its objectives and suggested that at the time, no suggested changes or additions to the original set of objectives were necessary. One member suggested that the task force objectives could be grouped into three categories: AACSB-related objectives, objectives pertaining to communication with Academy members and professional associations, and objectives pertaining to recommendations to the Academy's board of governors. The first task force meeting was perceived by members as being very useful in providing information, generating discussion, helping the task force become a working group, and providing a basis for identifying tasks (Albanese, 1988). Over the past two-and-a-half years several premises have evolved from the work of the Task Force on Outcome Measurement as they studied outcome measurement.

Premises Guiding the Task Force on Outcome Measurement

The following guiding premises are not intended to be chiseled in stone. However, they were intended to serve as a philosophical framework for guiding the preparation of the task forces's preliminary report for the board (submitted April 1990—final report was submitted to the board in August 1990) (Albanese, 1990):

1. The movement to develop and implement new approaches for assessing the student learning outcomes (i.e., knowledge and skills) of educational processes is a major development in higher education.

2. The movement to develop and implement outcome measures provides opportunities for business schools to further demonstrate their accountability. If business schools assume a leadership role in outcome measurement, the outcome measurement movement can serve important purposes.

3. The Academy of Management is uniquely qualified to play a leadership role in developing and implementing new approaches for assessing the outcomes of management educational processes.

4. The current interest and activity in outcome measurement by the AACSB is not an indicator of future change in the AACSB's accreditation process.

5. An institution's mission and goals are the beginning point for developing and implementing outcome measurement. Before meaningful outcome measurement can occur, schools will have to engage in a goal-setting process that identifies student learning goals that can be operationally measured.

6. The outcome measures used and the focus of outcome measures are multi-faceted. There is no one best approach for assessing the outcomes of educational processes.

7. Outcome measurement of management education suggests the importance of identifying a management "common body of knowledge" (CBK) and of developing reliable and valid CBK measures. While much management education is appropriately school specific, there are common elements of management education that cut across schools.

8. Variety and experimentation in developing and implementing outcome measures is essential. If outcome measurement is to be driven by a school's mission and goals, variety and experimentation should characterize the approaches used.

AACSB Task Force Findings on General Education Outcome Measurement

A large number of schools have adopted various types of outcome measures, including cognitive instruments, alumni and student questionnaires, attitude and personality instruments, and competency-based programs (Albanese and Dobbins, 1989). Most of these measures are designed to assess the extent to which the institution is meeting its overall educational goals. While the diversity of outcome measures is impressive, the psychometric characteristics of some of the instruments are a source of concern.

Cognitive measures such as the ACT-COMP or the ETS Academic Profile are the most common outcome measures of general education. These measures assess general intellectual skills such as solving problems, clarifying values, communicating within social institutions, and understanding technology.

Another common outcome measure of general education is alumni and student questionnaires. These questionnaires typically focus on the perceived quality of education, the effect that the institution had on personal development, and the extent to which educational experiences provided alumni with the skills necessary to work in their chosen fields. The most commonly used questionnaire is published by ACT's Evaluation/Survey Service, but many institutions have developed their own instruments. In addition, several institutions collect information through exit interviews with graduating seniors and follow-up interviews with alumni.

A smaller segment of colleges assess changes in student attitudes, their personalities, tolerance of others, and ethical reasoning. These institutions have mission statements which indicate that the educational process should help students grow morally, spiritually, and in their sense of civic responsibility. These institutions assess changes in students' values using instruments such as Altruism Scale, Responsibility Test, Myers-Brigg Type Indicator, Self-Esteem Questionnaire, and the Ethical Reasoning Test (Albanese and Dobbins, 1989).

Competency-based programs are used by a few schools, most notably Sterling College and Alverno College. These programs contain exercises, case studies, and senior projects. Specific skill domains (e.g., communication, problem solving) are assessed during performance of structured activities.

Outcome Measures in Business Schools

While outcome measures are less frequently used in business schools, a dramatic increase will probably occur in the near future due to the recent development of two standardized paper and pencil instruments (Albanese and Dobbins, 1989). ETS developed the Business Test to be published in April 1990. It attempts to cover the core business curriculum at various types of institutions. The test questions are designed to measure not only the student's knowledge of significant facts, concepts, theories, and methodology, but also his or her ability to apply this knowledge. The test contains sections on accounting, economics, management, quantitative business analysis, finance, marketing, legal and social environment, and international business. The participating institutions will receive scores for each of these areas; students will receive individual scores in accounting, economics, quantitative business analysis, and management, as well as an overall score. Furthermore, several sets of norms will be developed which will allow institutions to compare themselves to their peers. The expected cost of the Business Test is $14 per student.

A second standardized instrument for assessing the success of learning in a business school is the Core Curriculum Assessment Program (CCAP), developed as part of AACSB's Outcome Measurement Project by the American College Testing Program. This test assesses students' understanding of basic material in accounting, business environment and strategy, finance, organizational and behavioral areas, marketing, management information systems, and quantitative analysis/operations research. The CCAP is shorter than the Business Test and individual feedback is not provided to the students. Furthermore, norms are not available for the CCAP; therefore, comparisons with peer institutions are impossible. Instead, the CCAP is designed to assess changes in student learning over time at each institution.

Limitations of Outcome Measures in Business Schools

A couple of potential limitations of outcome measures should be recognized (Albanese and Dobbins, 1989). As outcome measures become widely available, the measures may guide the education process. Instead of institutions defining the outcomes that they wish to produce, they may simply accept the standardized measures as relevant criteria. Furthermore, while locally developed or tailored instruments may better assess an institution's unique mission or goals, such measures may be unacceptable to the public since the findings cannot be compared to peer institutions.

Another concern with outcome measurement is the potential reliance upon cognitive assessments. Competency-based performance measures (e.g., simulations, assessment center exercises) and instruments which assess reasoning, thinking, critical thought, and problem solving are less frequently used, even though they assess important criteria. In response to this criticism, Development Dimensions International has constructed a competency-based assessment center for AACSB which assesses ten competencies (leadership, oral communication/presentation skills, written communication, planning and organizing, information gathering, problem analysis, decision making, delegation and control, self-objectivity, and disposition to lead). Unfortunately, the cost of this simulation—$198 per student—is prohibitive for most institutions.

A final concern is that many institutions are not aware of the psychometric limitations of the instruments they are using nor the strong relationship between cognitive ability and performance on many outcome measures. Institutions need to become more sophisticated in their appreciation of psychometric principles if outcome measures are to be appropriately used and accurately interpreted.

REFERENCES

Academy of Management. (1988). Task force on outcome measurement. *The Academy of Management Newsletter,* 18(3), 9.

Albanese, R. (1988). Outcome measurement: Task force on outcome measurement holds first meeting. *Academy of Management Newsletter,* 18(4), 2-3.

Albanese, R. (1990). Outcome measurement: Premises guiding the task force on outcome measurement. *The Academy of Management News.* 20(2), 7-8.

Albanese, R., & Dobbins, G. H. (1989). Outcome measurement: An examination of outcome measurement in higher education. *The Academy of Management News,* 19(4), 12-13.

144 APPENDIX

Association of American Colleges. (1985). *Integrity in the college curriculum: A report to the academic community.* Washington, DC: Association of American Colleges.

Bernardin, H. J., & Albanese, R. (1990). Outcome measurement: A review of state policies toward outcome measurement in higher education. *The Academy of Management News,* 20(1), 3-4.

Commonwealth of Virginia. (1985). Senate Joint Resolution No. 125.

Commonwealth of Virginia. (1986). Senate Joint Resolution No. 83.

Commonwealth of Virginia. (1989). Senate Bill No. 534.

Ewell P. T., & Boyer, C. M. (1989). History and context: acting out assessment in the five states. Unpublished paper.

Ewell, P. T., & Boyer C. M. (1989). Mandating performance: five states encounter assessment. Unpublished paper.

Sims, S. J. (1989). *The origins and development of Virginia's student assessment policy: A case study.* Unpublished doctoral dissertation, The College of William and Mary, Williamsburg, Virginia.

State Council of Higher Education for Virginia. (1974). *The Virginia plan for higher education.*

State Council of Higher Education for Virginia. (1983). *The Virginia plan for higher education.*

State Council of Higher Education for Virginia. (1985). *The Virginia plan for higher education.*

State Council of Higher Education for Virginia. (1986). *The measurement of student achievement and the assurance of quality in Virginia higher education: To the governor and the general assembly of Virginia: Senate document No. 14.* Richmond, Virginia.

State Council of Higher Education for Virginia. (1987). *The Virginia plan for higher education.*

Study Group on the Condition of Excellence in American Higher Education. (1984). *Involvement in learning: realizing the potential of American higher education.* Washington, DC.

Bibliography

Academy of Management. (1988). Task force on outcome measurement. *The Academy of Management Newsletter*, 18(3), 9.

Adelman, C., & Alexander, R. J. (1982). *The self-evaluating institution: Practice and principles in the management of educational change.* New York: Methuen & Co.

Albanese, R. (1988). Outcome measurement: Task force on outcome measurement holds first meeting. *Academy of Management Newsletter*, 18(4), 2-3.

Albanese, R. (1990). Outcome measurement: Premises guiding the task force on outcome measurement. *The Academy of Management News*, 20(2), 7-8.

Albanese, R., & Dobbins, G. H. (1989). Outcome measurement: An examination of outcome measurement in higher education. *The Academy of Management News*, 19(4), 12-13.

Andrews, G. J. (1983). Adapting accreditation to new clients. In K.E. Young and others (Eds.), *Understanding accreditation.* San Francisco: Jossey-Bass, 342-357.

Andrews, G. J., and others. (1978). *Assessing nontraditional education.* (4 vols.) Washington, DC: Council on Postsecondary Accreditation.

Association of American Colleges. (1985). *Integrity in the college curriculum: A report to the academic community.* Washington, DC: Association of American Colleges.

Astin, A. W.; Bowens, H. R.; and Chambers, C. M. (1979). *Evaluating educational quality: A conference summary.* Washington, DC: Council on Postsecondary Accreditation.

Banta, T. W. (1989). Weaving assessment into the fabric of higher education. *Assessment Update,* 1(2), 3.

Bennett, W. J. (1984). *To reclaim a legacy: A report on the humanities in higher education.* Washington, DC: National Endowment for the Humanities.

Bennett, W. J. (1986). Text of Secretary Bennett's address last week at a Harvard University anniversary celebration. *The Chronicle of Higher Education,* 27-31.

Bergquist, W. H., & Armstrong, J. L. (1986). *Planning effectively for educational quality.* San Francisco: Jossey-Bass.

Bernardin, H. J. (1990). Outcomes measurement: A review of state policies toward outcome measurement in higher education. *The Academy of Management News,* 20(1), 3-4.

Bernardin, H. J., & Albanese, R. (1990). Outcome measurement: A review of state policies toward outcome measurement in higher education. *The Academy of Management News,* 20(1), 3-4.

Bernardin, H. J., & Ulrich, D. (1990). The measurement of student outcomes: State level activities (draft). An update of a 1986 report by Joni E. Finney and Carol M. Boyer.

Bloom, B. S.; Madaus, G. F.; & Hastings, J. T. (1981). *Evaluation to improve learning.* New York: McGraw-Hill Book Company.

Bok, D. (1979). The federal government and the university. *The Public Interest,* 50, 80-101.

Bok, D. (1986). Text of Harvard president Derek Bok's response to education secretary Bennett. *The Chronicle of Higher Education,* 17-19.

Bowens, H. R. (Ed.) (1974). *Evaluating institutions for accountability.* New Directions for Institutional Research. San Francisco: Jossey-Bass.

Boyer, C. M. (1985). *Five reports: Summary of the recommendations of recent commission reports on improving undergraduate education.* Education Commission of the States.

Boyer, C. M., & Ewell, P. T. (1988). *State-based case studies of assessment initiatives in undergraduate education: Chronol-*

ogy of critical points. Denver: Education Commission of the States.

Boyer, C. M.; Ewell, P. T.; Finney, J. E.; & Mingle, J. R. (1987). Assessment and outcomes measurement: A view from the states. *AAHE Bulletin.*

Bridger, G. (1989). Attitudinal surveys in institutional effectiveness. In J. O. Nichols (Ed.), *Institutional effectiveness and outcomes assessment implementation on campus: A practitioner's handbook.* New York: Agathon Press.

Brown, G. H., & Faupel, E. M. (1986). *Postsecondary assessment report of a planning conference November 20, 1986.* Center for Education Statistics. Office of Educational Research and Improvement. U.S. Department of Education.

Bunda, M. A. (1988). *Assessment and policy analysis in higher education.* A paper presented at the American Educational Research Association Annual Meeting, April, 1988. New Orleans.

Byham, W. C., & Thornton III, G. C. (1986). Assessment Centers. In Ronald A. Berk (Ed.), *Performance assessment: Methods and applications.* Baltimore: The Johns Hopkins University Press.

Campbell, D. T., & Stanley, J. C. (1979). *Experimental and quasi-experimental designs for research.* Chicago: Rand McNally College Publishing Company.

Commission on Colleges. (1981). Report of the subcommittee to survey the state of the art of outcomes assessment in higher education. Atlanta, GA: Southern Association of Colleges and Schools.

Commonwealth of Virginia. (1985). Senate Joint Resolution No. 125.

Commonwealth of Virginia. (1986). Senate Joint Resolution No. 83.

Commonwealth of Virginia. (1989). Senate Bill No. 534.

Cook, E. C. (1989). FIPSE's role in assessment: Past, present, and future. *Assessment Update,* 1(2), 1–3.

Cowan, D. (1984). The expanding conflict: Society's demands/academic independence. *Change,* 16(2), 34–39, 54.

Daft, R. L. (1989). *Organization theory.* New York: West Publishing Company.

Darling-Hammond, L. (1989). Accountability for professional practice. *Teacher College Record,* 91(1), 59–80.

Davis, B. G. (1989). Demistifying assessment: Learning from the field of evaluation. *Achieving assessment goals using evaluation techniques*. New Directions for Higher Education, no. 67. San Francisco: Jossey-Bass.

Dressel, P. T. (1949). *Comprehensive examinations in a program of general education*. East Lansing: Michigan State College Press.

Dressel, P. T., & Mayhew, L. B. (1954). *General education: Explorations in evaluation*. Washington, DC: American Council on Education.

Eckert, R. E. (1943). *Outcomes of general education: An appraisal of the general college program*. Minneapolis: The University of Minnesota Press.

Edgerton, R. (1986). An assessment of assessment. *Assessing the outcomes of higher education*. Proceedings of the ETS Invitational Conference. October 25, 1986.

El-Khawas, E. (1989). How are assessment results being used? *Assessment Update*, 1(4), 1–2.

Ewell, P. T. (1985). Editor's Notes. In P. T. Ewell (Ed.), *Assessing educational outcomes*. New Directions for Institutional Research, no. 47. San Francisco: Jossey-Bass.

Ewell, P. T. (1985). *Levers for change: The role of state government in improving the quality of postsecondary education*. Denver: Education Commission of the States.

Ewell, P. T. (1987). *Assessment, accountability and improvement: managing the contradiction*. AAHE Assessment Forum.

Ewell, P. T. (1987). Assessment: Where are we? *Change*, 19(1), 23–28.

Ewell, P. T., & Boyer, C. M. (1988). Acting out state-mandated assessment. *Change* 20(4), 41–47.

Ewell, P. T., & Boyer, C. M. (1989). History and context: acting out assessment in the five states. Unpublished paper.

Ewell, P. T., & Boyer C. M. (1989). Mandating performance: five states encounter assessment. Unpublished paper.

Federal Register, Department of Education. (1987). *34CFR Parts 602 and 603, Secretary's procedures and criteria for recognition of accrediting agencies; Notice of proposed rulemaking*. Washington, DC: Government Printing Office.

Federal Register, Department of Education. (1988). *34CFR Parts 602 and 603, Secretary's procedures and criteria for recognition of accrediting agencies; Final regulations.* Washington, DC: Government Printing Office.

Floyd, C. E. (1982). *State planning, budgeting, and accountability: Approaches for higher education.* AAHE-ERIC/Higher Education Research Report, no. 6.

Folger, J. K., and Harris, J. W. (1989). *Assessment in accreditation.* Sponsored by: A Grant from the Improvement of Postsecondary Education.

Finn, C. E. (1978). *Scholars, dollars, & bureaucrats.* Washington, DC.: The Brookings Institution.

Forrest, A. (1981). Outcome evaluation for revitalizing general education. In Jack Lindquist (Ed.), *Increasing the role of institutional research.* New Directions for Institutional Research, 32. San Francisco: Jossey-Bass.

Gambino, A. J. (1979). *Planning and control in higher education.* New York, N.Y.: National Association of Accountants.

Glazer, N. (1979). Regulating business and the universities: One problem or two? *The Public Interest,* 51, 43–65.

Harcleroad, F. F. (1980). *Accreditation: History, process, and problems.* AAHE-ERIC Higher Education Research Report, no. 6.

Harris, J. (1985). Assessing outcomes in higher education. In Clifford Adelman (Ed.), *Assessment in American higher education: Issues and contexts.* Washington, DC: Office of Educational Research and Improvement. U.S. Department of Education.

Hartle, T. W. (1985). The growing interest in measuring the educational achievement of college students. In Clifford Adelman (Ed.), *Assessment in American higher education: Issues and contexts.* Washington, DC: Office of Educational Research and Improvement. U.S. Department of Education.

Hawthorne, E. M. (1989). *Evaluating employee training programs: A research-based guide for human resource managers.* New York: Quorum Books.

Hellriegel, D., & Slocum, J. W. (1989). *Management* (fifth edition). Reading, Massachusetts: Addison-Wesley Publishing Company.

Heywood, J. (1977). *Assessment in higher education.* New York: John Wiley and Son.

Hutchings, P., & Marchese, T. (1990). Watching assessment: Questions, stories, prospects. *Change,* 22(5), 13–38.

150   BIBLIOGRAPHY

Jencks, C., & Riesman D. (1977). *The academic revolution.* Chicago: The University of Chicago Press.

Jordan, T. E. (1989). *Measurement and evaluation in higher education: Issues and illustrations.* New York: The Falmer Press.

Krotseng, M. (1989). Cognitive assessment instruments: Availability and utilization. In J. O. Nichols (Ed.), *Institutional effectiveness and outcomes assessment implementation on campus.* New York: Agathon Press.

Learned, W. S., & Wood, B. D. (1938). *The student and his knowledge: A report to the Carnegie Foundation on the results of the high school and college examinations of 1928, 1930, and 1932.* Bulletin no. 29. New York: Carnegie Foundation for the Advancement of Teaching.

Lenning, O. T. (1977). *Previous attempts to structure educational outcomes and outcomes related concepts: A compilation and review of the literature.* Boulder, Colorado: National Center for Higher Education Management Systems.

Lenning, O. T. (1980). Assessment and evaluation. In Ursula Delworth, Gary R. Hanson, and Associates (Eds.), *Student services: A handbook for the profession.* San Francisco: Jossey-Bass.

Levine, A. (1981). *Handbook on undergraduate curriculum.* San Francisco: Jossey-Bass Publishers.

Loacker, G. (1988). Faculty as a force to improve instruction through assessment. In J. H. McMillian (Ed.) *Assessing student's learning.* New Directions for Teaching and Learning, no. 34. San Francisco: Jossey-Bass.

Manning, T. E. (1988). Are the Secretary's intentions honorable? *Academe,* 74(4), 12–15.

MacLean, M. S. (1943). Forward to R. E. Eckert's *Outcomes of general education.* Minneapolis: The University of Minnesota Press.

McClain, C. J., & Krueger, D. W. (1985). Using outcomes assessment: A case study in institutional change. In Peter Ewell (Ed.), *Assessing educational outcomes.* New Directions for Institutional Research, no. 47. San Francisco: Jossey-Bass.

Marcus, L.; Leone, A. O. & Goldberg, E. D. (1983). *The path to excellence: Quality assurance in higher education.* AAHE-ERIC Higher Education Research Report, no. 1.

Micek, S. S., & Wallhaus, R. A. (1973). *An Introduction to the identification and uses of higher education outcome information.* T. R. 40. Boulder, Colorado: NCHEMS.

Miller, R. I. (1980). *The assessment of college performance.* San Francisco: Jossey-Bass Publishers.

Miller, R. I. (1988). Using Change Strategies to Implement Assessment Programs. In T. W. Banta's (Ed.) *Implementing Outcomes Assessment: Promise and Perils.* New Directions for Institutional Research, no. 59. San Francisco: Jossey-Boss.

Morante, E. A. (1986) The state of the states in postsecondary assessment. *Postsecondary assessment report of a planning conference November 20, 1986.* Center for Education Statistics. Office of Educational Research and Improvement. U.S. Department of Education.

National Commission on Excellence in Education. (1983). *A nation at risk: The imperative for educational reform.* Washington, DC: U.S. Department of Education.

National Governors' Association. (1986). *Time for results: The governors' 1991 report on education.* Washington, DC: The National Governor's Association.

National Institute of Education. (1984). *Involvement in learning: Realizing the potential of American higher education.* Washington, DC: National Institute of Education.

Nichols, J. O. (1989). *Institutional effectiveness and outcomes assessment implementation on campus: A practitioners handbook.* New York: Agathon Press.

Pace, C. R. (1979). *Measuring the outcomes of college.* San Francisco: Jossey-Bass.

Pace, C. R. (1984). Historical perspectives on student outcomes: Assessment with implications for the future. *NASPA Journal,* 22(2), 10–18.

Packer, A. (1989). Preparing the workforce 2000. *Human Capital,* 1(1), 34–38.

Palmer, S. E. (1986). Education secretary calls for fundamental changes in colleges. *The Chronicle of Higher Education,* 1, 27.

Palmer S. E. (1986). Campus officials assail Bennett's attack on colleges; Harvard's Bok Calls Secretary's Analysis 'Superficial.' *The Chronicle of Higher Education,* 1, 17.

Pike, G. R. (1989). Assessment measures. *Assessment Update*, 1(2), 8–9.

Pratt, L.; Reichard, D.; & Rogers, B. (1989). Designing the assessment process. In J. O. Nichols (Ed.), *Institutional effectiveness and outcomes assessment implementation on campus.* New York: Agathon Press.

Raoul, A. A. (1983). Establishing successful faculty evaluation and development programs. In A. Smith (Ed.), *Evaluating faculty and staff.* New Directions in Community Colleges, 41. San Francisco: Jossey-Bass.

Resnick, D., & Goulden, M. (1987). Assessment, curriculum and expansion in American higher education: A historical perspective. In Diane Halpern (Ed.), *Student outcomes assessment: What institutions stand to gain.* New Directions in Higher Education, no. 59, XV(3).

Rossmann, J. E., & El-Khawas, E. (1987). *Thinking about assessment: Perspectives for presidents and chief academic officers.* Washington, DC: American Association for Higher Education. American Council on Education.

Selden, W. K. (1960). *Accreditation: A struggle over standards in higher education.* New York: Harper and Bros.

Sell, G. R. (1989). Making assessment work: A synthesis and future directions. In Peter J. Gray (Ed.), *Achieving assessment goals using evaluation techniques.* New Directions for Higher Education, no. 67. San Francisco: Jossey-Bass.

Sharp, B. H. (1989). Assessment related information from institutional data systems. In J. O. Nichols (Ed.), *Institutional effectiveness and outcomes assessment implementation on campus.* New York: Agathon Press.

Shils, E. (1983). *The academic ethic.* Chicago: University of Chicago Press.

Sims, S. J. (1989). *The origins and development of Virginia's student assessment policy: A case study.* Unpublished doctoral dissertation, The College of William and Mary, Williamsburg, Virginia.

Southern Association of Colleges and Schools. (1987). *Resource manual on institutional effectiveness.* Commission on Colleges.

Staff. (1985). Bennett calls on colleges to assess their own performance, publish results. *Chronicle of Higher Education*, 25.

SCHEV. (1974). *The Virginia plan for higher education.*
SCHEV. (1983). *The Virginia plan for higher education.*
SCHEV. (1985). *The Virginia plan for higher education.*
SCHEV. (1986). *The measurement of student achievement and the assurance of quality in Virginia higher education: To the governor and the general assembly of Virginia: Senate document No. 14.* Richmond, Virginia.
SCHEV. (1987). *The Virginia plan for higher education.*
State of Florida Department of Education (1984-85). *Questions & Answers about college and academic skills tests in community colleges and state universities.*
Study Group on the Condition of Excellence in American Higher Education. (1984). *Involvement in learning: Realizing the potential of American higher education.* Washington, DC.
Thrash, P. A. (1988). Educational outcomes in the accrediting process. *Change, 74*(4), 16–18.
Tracey, W. R. (1968). *Evaluating training and development systems.* United States of America: American Management Association, Inc.
Trivett, D. A. (1976). *Accreditation and institutional eligibility.* ERIC/Higher Education Research Report, no. 9.
Tyler, R. W. (1947). Forward to the Executive Committee of the Cooperative Study in General Education's *Cooperation in General Education.* Washington, DC: American Council on Education.
W & M (1986). *Student assessment plan.*
Wergin, J. (1989). Politics of assessment in the university. *Assessment Update, 1*(2), 5–7.
Wildavsky, A. (1979). *Speaking truth to power: The art and craft of policy analysis.* Boston: Little, Brown & Company.
Young, K. E. (1983). The changing scope of accreditation. In K.E. Young and others (Eds.), *Understanding accreditation.* San Francisco: Jossey-Bass.

Index

Accountability, 10–12, 73, 77, 110; defined, 10; higher education and, 17–18; political, 15–16; states and, 16–17

Accreditation: defined, 65; historical roles of, 68–79; purpose of, 65–67; state mistrust of, 50–51

Accrediting agencies: institutional protector, 68–71; Middle Atlantic Association of Schools and Colleges, 68; New England Association of Schools and Colleges, 68, 69; North Central Association of Colleges and Universities, 68, 69; Northwest Association of Schools and Colleges, 68; outcomes assessment, 73–78; professional associations, 70, 73; quality of accrediting standards, 71–73; roles of, 68–78; Southern Association of Colleges and Schools, 68, 69; Western Asso-

ciation of Colleges and Universities, 68

ACT Comp, 58–59

Alverno College, 37–38, 55; assessment centers and, 37–38

American Assembly of Collegiate Schools of Business, Task Force on Outcome Measurement, 56

American Council on Education, survey, 18

Assessment: context for, 10–12; defined, 4–5; design, 111–113; evaluation, 113–118; history, 12–13; implementation, 111–113; political forces for, 15–16; significance of, 4

Assessment centers, defined, 37–38

Assessment programs: designing, 83, 111–113; evaluating, 113–118; implementing, 83, 111–113

Assessment results: audiences for, 86, 87–89; uses of, 86–87, 103

About the Author

SERBRENIA J. SIMS has worked for the School of Education at the College of William and Mary and the Center for Government and Public Affairs at the Montgomery campus of Auburn University. She has published several articles on higher education and personnel training and co-edited (with Ronald R. Sims) *Managing Institutions of Higher Education into the 21st Century* (Greenwood Press, 1991).